LIVING IN
SMALL SPACES

LIVING IN
SMALL SPACES

LORRIE MACK

CONRAN OCTOPUS

Dedication
To my mum

Author's acknowledgments
My grateful thanks to Jackie Douglas and Roger Bristow for inspiring this book; to
Tristram Holland and Sarah Bevan for their belief in it and their support and
loyalty through tough times; to Carolline Murray for her boundless creativity and
enthusiasm; to Shona Wood for finding beautiful pictures to illustrate the text
before I had written it; to Dave Allen for turning impossible ideas into practical
projects; and finally, to Mary Davies for her outstandingly sensitive handling of the
manuscript and the author.

First published in 1988 by
Contran Octopus Limited
37 Shelton Street
London WC2H 9HN

This paperback edition published in 1992 by Conran Octopus Limited

Reprinted 1992

Project Editor	Mary Davies
Copy Editor	Penny David
Art Editor	Caroline Murray
Picture Research	Shona Wood
Production	Louise Barratt
	Jill Embleton
Technical Consultant	Dave Allen
Illustrations	Steve Cross
	John Woodcock

FRONTISPIECE: *A simple Victorian
desk provides a place to deal with
household paperwork in this small
living room; tiny corner shelves behind
it hold books and files.*

Typeset by Vantage Typesetters Limited
Printed and bound in Hong Kong

ISBN 1 85029 358 9

CONTENTS

TAKING STOCK

With property values soaring and accommodation becoming more and more scarce, people everywhere are having to adjust to living in increasingly small spaces. Like all restrictions however, this one can encourage great resourcefulness and creativity; it can focus attention on your needs and tastes and help you to recognize the potential of your rooms as well as their limitations. With imagination and careful planning, you can make every part of your home so comfortable and attractive that the reaction it inspires in visitors is not so much, 'What a clever use of space', as 'What a lovely room'.

Assessing your needs

To create this impression, first work out what your needs are and where your problems lie. Look at the lives of your home's occupants. What activities do they carry on there? Do they relax and entertain at home, or spend most of their time elsewhere? Does anyone work from home? How many and what kind of belongings does each person need to accommodate?

Next, establish your priorities, making sure, for example, that any regular, time-consuming pursuit is allotted its own space so equipment does not have to be cleared away repeatedly to free the area for other uses. Similarly, think about which items you use most frequently in every room, so they can have first call on easily accessible storage areas. Don't rush to make 'improvements' without thinking them through – fitting every spare corner with cupboards and shelves is not the best solution if additional work surfaces are what is really needed in your home.

Try to identify those situations that need attention because they make you feel particularly cramped and jostled. Is there constant conflict over use of the bathroom? Does everyone pile into the living room at the same time? Do you regret not being able to put up overnight visitors? Are you desperate for a corner you can have to yourself? Does someone's space-consuming hobby constantly have to be cleared off the dining table or the floor?

Surveying your resources

Before you contemplate any great changes, see what you can gain by re-examining all your present

RIGHT *Even when it's not possible to improve your home by altering its structure or acquiring special furniture and fittings, you can create the illusion of greater space using decorative elements like colour, pattern and light.*

arrangements. Evaluate the contents of every room and cast aside any item that is not there for a very good reason. Extreme sentiment may justify holding on to a few useless pieces, but habit does not – no chair or table should take up precious space simply because you have always had it, you were given it, or you bought it cheaply and it's still in one piece. Nor should blind adherence to furnishing tradition qualify any article for house room – nowhere is it written that you must own a toaster or a dining table or a chest of drawers if you think you can manage perfectly well without.

Once you are aware of what you have and what you need, you are ready to take action, and there are three main tactics at your disposal: you can alter the fabric of your home to make it bigger; you can organize the existing space to make the best use of it; and you can employ decorative elements like colour, pattern and lighting to give the impression of space. Clearly, the choices you make will depend on the degree of commitment in time and energy, as well as cash, you are prepared to give, but the ideas and information in this book will make it possible to improve any environment dramatically.

Adapting your outlook

You'll be happier in your small home if you accept a few compromises. Some items – preferably seldom-used ones – will inevitably get housed in inconvenient places. Some activities – entertaining very large numbers perhaps – will have to be curtailed.

However anarchic your domestic arrangements have been in the past, you should discipline yourself to be reasonably organized: to put things away when you've finished with them, to hang up your clothes each night, to tidy the kitchen after meals. Cultivating these habits can make an enormous difference to the quality of life in a restricted area, especially when more than one person lives there.

Finally, use every resource available to plan and decorate your home to suit your needs and your tastes, but don't let it become a showplace for designer gimmicks. The most important criterion for any element of furnishing or decoration is whether you are happy with it.

LEFT *Provide a simply-constructed work area in a student's bedroom, so books and papers don't have to be cleared regularly from the dining table. Here, roomy cupboards under the bed help to compensate for the resulting loss of storage space.*

RIGHT *If constant traffic is a problem in the family kitchen, fit out a spare corner elsewhere with the necessary equipment and supplies for preparing snacks and informal meals. This U-shaped unit tucked under the basement stairs is ideal.*

GUIDELINES
FOR SUCCESS

The first step in coping with a cramped environment is to

consider the space in your home as a whole. Start by taking a

fresh look at the potential for change and adaptation in its

overall arrangement, then sort out your structural detailing

and services, and finally move on to the decorative devices

that create the all-important *feeling* of space.

The conventional way of allotting functions to rooms in a family home – living room on the ground floor, bedrooms upstairs; master bedroom for parents, secondary ones for children, and so on – may not result in the best possible use of space. Bearing in mind *all* the available space, take a fresh look at these traditional arrangements to see whether a more flexible approach might liberate under-used areas, or enable you to combine different functions in the same room.

If the biggest and brightest room in the house is one of the upstairs bedrooms, for example, make this into the living room since it is probably large enough to accommodate several activity areas, and turn the smaller ground-floor space into a bedroom. Or just swap bedrooms, letting the children have the big one as a sleeping-plus-play area, thus freeing the living room.

If you work at home in a one-bedroom flat or apartment, or if you pursue a space- or time-consuming hobby there, combine your living and sleeping quarters in the larger room and release the smaller one

for full-time office or studio use. Aside from using space more effectively and avoiding the need to clear away all relevant paraphernalia regularly, this reorganization gives you the considerable psychological advantages of a separate work area.

If you have no need for extensive cooking facilities and your living room is a good size, install a stylish kitchen area at one end. Indeed, if your home consists of one room plus separate kitchen and bathroom, this plan can free the kitchen to make a tiny bedroom or even a large walk-in cupboard, which would take an enormous amount of pressure off the main living area.

You may find that a change of use, as well as saving space, will enable you to take advantage of increased light at the time of day when the room is most occupied, or to enjoy an especially pretty view. Small-space dwellers, who have few rooms to live in or little chance of rearranging the furniture, might try switching the functions of rooms around from time to time simply to provide a change of scene; it also helps to equalize wear.

PAGE 10 *Separate off a kitchen corner with a peninsular unit and a smart venetian blind.*

LEFT *This large half-landing has been turned into an office by lining it with storage shelves hidden by sliding panels, then boxing it in with folding doors. The architect who works here*

has made these into a changing portfolio of his work.

RIGHT *Make one end of a spacious living room into a compact kitchen, an arrangement that lends itself to many stylistic interpretations. The original kitchen can then be adapted for another use.*

LEFT *Many flat conversions are in old houses with lofty ceilings, under which you could build a gallery. Even if this is too low to make living or sleeping quarters, it might do as a library, study, guest room or storage area. If carving up a large space has resulted in a small room with a too-high ceiling, such a gallery may even help to improve its proportions.*

If you cannot reorganize the existing rooms in your home to meet your space requirements, investigate the possibility of making some degree of structural change. Although this can be both expensive and inconvenient, it is almost certainly less so than moving to a larger place. Before undertaking any major alteration, however, you must seek specialist advice; you must also obtain any necessary planning permission *before* the work is begun. Make sure, too, that any changes you are considering (like reducing the number of bedrooms by knocking two together) will not limit the flexibility and therefore the appeal of your home, making it more difficult to sell when the time comes, and are sympathetic to the character of the building.

Exploiting unused areas

Look carefully at every part of your home that is not currently being used as living space – the attic, the basement, the garage and any area designated for long-term storage, since the very existence of such a

place actually encourages hoarding.

Attics and basements are traditional areas for home expansion (they are covered in more detail on pages 106–107), but it's becoming increasingly popular to convert an integral garage in the same way. Usually large and conveniently located, this space might make an ideal kitchen, study or extra bedroom, and you could easily provide a separate entrance here, offering greater privacy to the occupant and reducing congestion in the main part of the house. Many garages have only electricity laid on, so you may have to provide insulation, heating and plumbing, but the cost will still be far less than building an extension, and you'll have no worries about how well it blends in with the rest of the house.

Potential for change

One of the best ways to improve the efficiency of a small home is by reducing congestion in the bathroom. See if you can squeeze in an extra shower or toilet somewhere – under the stairs perhaps, in a hall, on a landing or in the corner of a bedroom. If two adjacent bedrooms have large adjoining cupboards, knock them through to create a small second bathroom that will save frayed tempers during the morning rush.

Consider the connecting areas, the halls and stairs everyone has to pass through to get from one place to another. Maybe the stairs could be moved to another location, or replaced with some of a different design – dog-leg or spiral, for example. It might be possible to create extra space, or to re-route traffic along a more convenient path.

Look at the windows and external doors to see if you can gain anything by switching their positions. Open up a window to make a new back or side door, thus re-routing traffic, then fill in the bottom of the existing doorway to make the space around it more useable. You may decide to remove the second door altogether, releasing space and improving security at the same time.

Impressions of space

In terms of increasing the *feeling* of light and space in your environment, simply enlarging small windows could make an enormous improvement. Another obvious way is by removing internal walls. Older homes were often divided into small rooms to retain warmth, but since most now have central heating, this is no longer necessary.

RIGHT *This top-floor retreat was poky and boring until its owner added height and interest by opening it up to expose the roof beams, later picked out in green to emphasize the room's unusual shape. White walls and coir matting add to the feeling of spaciousness, and provide a perfect backdrop for an exotic collection of rugs, pictures and tapestries.*

Get rid of a long, narrow (and often wasted) entrance hall by knocking it through to the adjacent living room, perhaps keeping a low wall to divide the area visually, contain any wiring, cut draughts and provide a vertical surface against which to position furniture. Probably the most common alteration of this type combines the living and dining rooms, the latter being a luxury few small-space occupants can afford. If your dining room adjoins a tiny kitchen, you might prefer to make these two rooms into a single, larger one instead.

Opening up your home like this will certainly make it feel less cramped and poky, but again, it's important that you weigh up all your priorities before you make your decisions. If there are several people in the household, you might find that their collective longing for wide open spaces is less pressing than their individual needs for peace, privacy and quiet.

One dramatic alteration that does not affect the home's internal divisions, however, is to transform a boxy bungalow by knocking out part of the attic floor and insulating the roof right under the rafters to give a soaring, cathedral-like ceiling in the living room.

Building on

The most obvious way of making more space is to build on some form of extension – outwards into the garden or upwards through the roof. A small home will probably not have a huge amount of space in which to expand, so you may have to make some sacrifices for the greater good. If there is a garden or patio, evaluate honestly how much you use it and consider enclosing at least part of it to extend your permanently useable living area.

Much less ambitious than a home extension, a tiny but attractively constructed shed in the garden, as long as it's dry and secure, would cope with suitcases, sports equipment, out-of-season clothes, paint tins and tools – anything that is not in constant use yet bulky to store. With power laid on, it might even serve as a workshop or study.

FAR LEFT *You can sometimes alleviate congestion in areas of heavy traffic by re-locating a flight of stairs. The wall that originally divided these off has been replaced with a row of thin wooden battens, which define each area while allowing light to pass through and giving an un-interrupted wall-to-wall view. Use the same tactic to separate activity areas in a large bedsitter, studio or loft, or hang vertical louvred blinds.*

LEFT *Once the master bedroom of a Victorian merchant's home, this large first-floor chamber had later been carved up with a stud wall. When the building was converted into flats, it was a simple task to remove this, and install a single kitchen-dining-living space in the original room, which is outstandingly airy and light; the pretty arch and slim black columns divide living and dining areas without having any structural function. Removing a load-bearing wall however, is much more complex and difficult, since you will have to replace it with another means of support in the form of a joist, beam or truss.*

RIGHT *Enjoy the advantages of both a garden and a patio by adding on a well-built conservatory that is heated and insulated so you can eat, work and relax in it all year round. With its prettily-shaped green frame and glazing bars (and the natural colours and textures inside), this one makes a natural link between the house and the garden.*

Before you begin to decorate and furnish, give careful thought to the structural detailing we often take for granted. Minor components that can go unnoticed in generously proportioned rooms are mercilessly exposed or become major inconveniences in diminutive ones.

Doors

How many of your internal doors are absolutely necessary? Clearly those on the bathroom and bedroom are there to ensure peace and seclusion, but if the constant traffic in and out of the kitchen or living room means their doors are continually open, remove them altogether. You can then make use of every bit of wall space, and plan the rest of the room without having to accommodate door clearance.

If you are unwilling to leave your rooms completely open, replace conventional doors with sliding or folding ones that take up far less space, or hang curtains that can be pulled across to conceal mess or afford privacy. You may be able to make better use of space in a room or its adjoining hall or landing by rehanging the existing door to open out instead of in, or vice versa.

Power

An often-overlooked detail is the location and number of electrical outlets. Installing several in every wall before you decorate will justify the cost and inconvenience since it allows you to position table lamps, stereo, television and video recorder anywhere in the living room or bedroom without worrying about dangerously trailing flexes or cords. Such flexibility is particularly vital in the kitchen, where safety and convenience are so important.

Heating

When you are trying to arrange the furniture in an undersized room so it looks tidy and uses all the available space, it's surprising how often you are frustrated by the ill-conceived positioning of several

LEFT Free floor and wall surfaces and expand space visually by removing unnecessary doors altogether. In a kitchen, try fixing saloon-type swing panels in the middle of the frame, which would achieve a similar effect, yet hide dirty dishes.

RIGHT To increase light in your home dramatically, replace solid doors with those containing clear glass panels. Glazed internal doors will give an impression of greater space while cutting noise levels and maintaining maximum insulation.

radiators. Altering your heating system to a greater or lesser degree, although it may be costly, could increase your actual or apparent space dramatically.

The simplest option is to reposition the existing radiators to free additional – or even just more useful – floor area. Since an alarming number of heating systems seem to be installed with no thought or planning whatsoever, this should not be difficult. If you are willing to go to slightly more trouble, consider replacing your radiators with those of a different design, like the several skirting or baseboard versions widely available. Slim and unobtrusive, these are fixed around the room just above floor level and allow you to position your furniture almost anywhere you like. You will get nearly as much flexibility by choosing stylish, wall-mounted models that can be fixed vertically instead of horizontally. One of the most ingenious solutions of all to the warmth-vs-space problem is the installation of a vertical model in the middle of the floor as a room divider. Old-fashioned large, bulky radiators are

LEFT Available in a huge range of sizes, colours and designs, many modern radiators can be fixed in the centre of a room as well as along a wall. In this smart bathroom, a bright, sculptural model divides off the shower area and acts as a heated towel rail as well as warming the room.

still available from speciality outlets, and you could consider fixing one of these in such a position to define space in a bedsitter or loft.

The most drastic measure you can take – and one that is suitable only for new homes, extensions or major refurbishments – is to put in an entirely new heating system, such as one of those that run either under the floor or above the ceiling, taking up no space at all. Although not quite as convenient and space-saving, ducted warm-air systems work by blowing the heat into each area through grilles strategically positioned in the walls.

At the other end of the scale, in short-term accommodation or buildings where the installation of central heating is impractical, the most appropriate heat source is a portable electrical appliance of the radiant type, or the convector type that can be placed on the floor, hung on the wall or set into the plinth at the base of a kitchen unit. Fairly cheap to buy, these are expensive to run since they use a great deal of energy, and of course they lack much of the convenience of whole-house systems.

There is one freestanding heating element on the market, however, that offers many advantages. Much costlier initially than ordinary electric fires and heaters, this is a small (15cm, 6in), light, square box that plugs into an electrical outlet in the usual way. Its revolutionary characteristic is that it is thermostatically controlled so it stays on all the time, maintaining the room at a constant temperature without adjustment. The unit is also much safer than standard heating appliances, since it remains cool to the touch.

Sound barriers

Remember that one of the most profound irritations of small-space living is the intrusion of other people's noise. On the whole, it is much easier to contain loudness in the room of its origin than to keep it out of any other area, so retain barrier doors in a family dwelling, and improve sound insulation generally by laying carpet and underlay in all the rooms and on any stairs, landings or halls. Line the walls of relevant rooms – a teenager's bedroom that contains a stereo perhaps, or one where a noisy hobby is carried on – with cork or fabric-covered softboard on which mementoes can be pinned.

If raucous neighbours are your problem, putting these measures into operation will bring you some peace, but getting on good enough terms so you can encourage them to do the same is even more effective.

RIGHT *A solid run of shelves filled with books or records acts as an extremely efficient layer of sound insulation. Cover the wall behind them with cork, softboard or thick fabric to muffle music or the noise from a television, typewriter or sewing machine even more effectively.*

The most effective way to give your home a feeling of space and harmony is to work out one basic decorating scheme, then keep it the same, or very similar, throughout, so that no vista is interrupted by changes of colour and pattern.

Cover all your floors with the same – or at least the same colour – material: if beige carpet is your choice in the living room, bedroom and hall, fix vinyl or quarry tiles of a matching tone in the kitchen and bathroom. Go for an all-over treatment in each area, rather than rugs laid on a contrasting floor covering, which will shrink the room visually. If you want small rugs in areas of heavy wear, look for those in a similar tone to the carpet or wood underneath.

Ideally, stick to the same shade, or a closely related one, for all the walls and ceilings, the window coverings and even the major items of furniture. Keep in mind that slight variations in the colour of the walls from room to room can go unnoticed, as they are separated by door frames, whereas carpet looks ugly when two different designs are joined at each threshold.

If every area in your home receives a similar decorative treatment, you will also gain flexibility, since the accessories and minor items of furniture that add interest can easily be moved from room to room periodically.

Carry the principle of creating unbroken surfaces through to your furnishing schemes: if you need shelves, fit them floor to ceiling rather than in twos and threes in the middle of a wall. Choose curtains that run from floor to ceiling as well, or even across one whole wall.

Pull every part of your home together with common details: skirting boards (baseboards) and cornices, door knobs and light switches. For a subtly consistent look, run a delicate border along

every wall at floor or ceiling level. You could even choose all the storage units you need from the same range – a sturdy wooden or plastic cube system for example – so you can move individual pieces around according to need or whim.

If your windows don't vary dramatically in size, choose the same treatment for all of them – classic roller blinds perhaps, for a modern scheme, or simple curtains or shutters for a traditional one.

LEFT *Nothing breaks up space more than a warren of connecting areas, each decorated differently. This hall and the rooms leading off it are pulled together with white paint and floor tiles, which carry on up the kitchen walls. Note the well-planned storage area under the stairs.*

BELOW *Unappealing features such as radiators, pipes and bumpy walls can be camouflaged with decorative paint finishes like sponging or dragging.*

RIGHT *The convention of painting a ceiling white (rather than the same colour as the walls) often has little to recommend it. This attic room's awkward shape has been softened by using the same shade on the blind, as well as the walls and ceiling.*

Before you decide on a decorating style, consider first the kind of environment you are actually happiest living in; you may prefer 'busy' or womb-like surroundings, so don't automatically assume all small rooms demand a cool and sleek look.

The style of your home should suit your personality and your way of life as well as your aesthetic sensibilities. The pictures you adore in magazines may be spare and stark, showing white surfaces everywhere relieved only by one or two exquisite *objets*, but be realistic. Small spaces are subject to heavy wear, so if you are naturally untidy, if you have children or pets, or if your modest home must accommodate several people and activities, you'll either have to make some kind of compromise with a more human scheme, or spend your life tidying away clutter, scrubbing walls, floors and furniture and feeling irritated by the imperfect state of your surroundings.

Avoid the temptation to indulge in a bizarre, joky or exceptionally exotic scheme, since you'll have to

LEFT *When family activities centre around one room, it's vital that the colours and patterns you choose for decorations and furnishings provide a relaxing atmosphere, and one that you won't tire of quickly. Here, a glass table and perspex fire-guard look neat and unobtrusive, yet are practical and hardwearing in use.*

live with it every day, for a long time after the novelty has worn off.

Whereas people with large homes can afford to furnish some rooms in a style chosen only for its appearance, in smaller dwellings every room must meet your criteria for comfort as well as taste. If delicate French antiques or brutal modernist pieces are your fantasy, try to tone it down a little so you can also install comfortable sofas and chairs in which to relax.

Take into account too, the architectural character of your home. Space restrictions do not necessarily impose limitations on decorating style, but you should choose one that has a general sympathy with the shape, height and decorative detailing of your rooms. Massive formal pieces of furniture – however useful they might be for storage – can look out of place in poky or quirkily shaped rooms, whereas the open-plan layout of a studio is likely to swamp a dainty, cottage-inspired theme.

Whatever look you finally choose for your home, don't adhere to it slavishly; rooms should not be like paintings, complete and perfect in themselves. They are, in the end, only a setting for people and their lives. If you decorate them too obsessively, matching every cushion and lampshade and arranging symmetrical patterns, the effect you create will not only look contrived, it will automatically be ruined as soon as you walk in.

ABOVE *If you're happy in cosy, dark surroundings, play up the enclosed feeling of a small space rather than attempting to overcome it. This inviting box bed offers warmth and security on a sailing barge, but the effect would be easy to duplicate on dry land. Fix roomy cupboards above and below it to provide extra storage capacity for large or unwieldy items.*

LEFT *A fresh, all-white scheme will make almost any room look sunny and spacious, but if there are children (or less-than-tidy adults) using it constantly, make sure all materials and surfaces are easy to clean, and be prepared to devote a little time and energy to keeping everything in pristine condition.*

Colour is a powerful design tool: it can alter the apparent size and brightness of rooms and affect the way we feel in them.

Fooling the eye

One of the most basic rules is that light colours make spaces look larger, while darker ones have the opposite effect. So, clearly, if you want to increase the apparent size of small rooms, decorate with pale shades. It's also true that light surfaces seem to recede, darker ones to come closer in, and one often-delivered piece of advice is to paint your ceiling in a lighter shade than the walls to make it seem higher, or a deeper one to bring it down. This is probably worth doing only if your ceiling is extraordinarily high or low, in which case the effect will be much more natural if you extend the colour down to your picture- or plate-rail. (If there isn't one there, fix a length of beading or a wallpaper border.) On the whole though, your rooms will appear much more pulled together if these surfaces are treated the same.

Take advantage of the fact that pale colours reflect the light by using warm pastel tones in any room that is particularly dark – or one that is dark at the time of day you normally use it.

Altering mood

Colour has a profound effect on feelings, so never choose one you are not naturally drawn to because

RIGHT In a small room, use colour to camouflage a large piece of furniture like this capacious dresser (hutch), whose pretty mirrors reflect light and space in a tiny kitchen. In the same way, you could bring a huge sofa down to size by covering it to match the walls, curtains or blind behind it.

BELOW RIGHT When light is scarce, a warm colour like yellow, pink or peach is often a better choice than white, which can look grey and dingy.

FAR RIGHT If you want your home to be stimulating rather than restful, decorate with clear, bright colours. Subtly-striped wallpaper in sunny yellow, plus streaming light and full-length mirrors, make this bold holiday caravan seem much bigger than it is.

it's fashionable or unusual, or because it goes with a piece of furniture or a pair of curtains you already have. Take into consideration the 'mood' of each one – variations of red, yellow and orange are stimulating and aggressive (as are brilliant hues and dramatic contrasts), whereas cool colours like blue and green have a calming effect. Accordingly, try to plan your rooms around the atmosphere you require from your home. The designer tactic of using a neutral, all-over background allows you to pick different-coloured accessories for each room with this in mind and change the accent colours periodically for a fresh look.

To create lively, exciting rooms, however small, explore the different effects that can be achieved with pattern and texture.

Pattern potential

Since rooms look bigger decorated in plain colours, when you do choose patterns and prints make sure they have something positive to contribute. These can be employed in two ways: as a room's main decorative feature, or to provide areas of colour and accent in a simpler scheme. A large, dominant pattern would swamp most small rooms, but a small-scale one can sometimes be used to great effect. A subtly-striped wall covering for example, hung horizontally or vertically, will increase the apparent proportions of a room and, on a smaller scale, the same design used for curtain fabric can make a window look higher or wider. Draped over a large table, striped fabric could even appear to have an effect on the room's length or width.

Pattern, like colour, can be used very effectively as camouflage. Reduce the visual bulk of a favourite sofa by positioning it in front of a window and covering it in the same print as the curtains or blind. Even a huge boxy wardrobe would not look out of place in a small bedroom if it were papered all over to match the walls.

Don't be afraid to mix patterns, as long as you go carefully. If you are unsure of your own eye, select fabrics and wallpapers from the same range, or stick to small-scale designs in a similar style (geometric, flowery, and so on) and general family of colour (pastels, primaries, or soft, muted shades).

Texture tricks

Although fundamentally monochromatic rooms are the wisest choice when you want to make the most of available light and space, they can very easily end up looking flat and boring rather than subtle and tasteful. To get the most from one-colour schemes, explore the wide variety of available textures: knobbly wool, crispy lace and linen, slubby silk, matt cotton, coarse tweed, glossy plastic. You

can even make textures work for you: smooth light-reflecting paint exaggerating the illusion of space; coarse-textured wallpaper camouflaging uneven surfaces.

Make use of contrast in texture for maximum appeal; set a glass table on a velvety carpet or an intricately crocheted cushion on a polished wooden chest.

ABOVE *Use a pale, small-patterned paper to minimize awkward angles and corners, like the ones in this diminutive, but charming, attic bedroom. The same print has been used on the walls, at the window (on the sill and reveals as well as the blind), and over the bed, which completely fills the short arm of the room's difficult L-shape. (For a similarly unifying effect, cover a sloping ceiling or even a row of bookshelves in the same way.) To make the bed platform look built-in, it has been papered to match the walls, then finished off with a strip of skirting, matched to the room's own. Coir matting and cane furniture prevent the pattern repetition from deadening the scheme.*

ABOVE *Blue and white striped paper gives a cool, elegant feel to this modest bathroom, and makes it appear higher than it really is. The linear theme is echoed both in the wooden shutters, and the distinctive way they filter the light. Experiment with materials at a sunny window to see a range of effects; lace, for example, makes a pretty,* *dappled pattern, whereas cane breaks up light in a random diffused way.*

RIGHT *This inviting corner needs no dramatic tricks to achieve its charm. The shapes and textures of the objects – delicate flowers, glowing wood, shiny brass and silver, cool marble, woven tapestry – are more than enough.*

The treatment you choose for your windows not only alters the apparent size of your rooms, it also affects that most precious of all commodities in a small space – light. Whatever decorating style you've chosen, try to avoid fussy or overblown effects. Huge, heavy curtains, relentlessly frilly blinds and any style that involves intricate borders, bows, swags or tassels all risk creating an impression of clutter and muddle, and so minimizing the space visually. Go for unadorned curtains, blinds or even shutters, in a colour or pattern that does not contrast dramatically with the surrounding walls.

Treated separately, two or more windows in the same wall – especially if they're different sizes – can make a room look bitty and jumbled. For a simple, unifying effect, cover the whole window area with a single pair of curtains or even with one large blind.

Blinds

Where the plainest possible treatment is called for, or when even wall space is at a premium, blinds or shades of one kind or another are the neatest window-covering. They also save the day if you find short curtains too cottagey, yet have radiators fixed under windows, rendering full-length ones impractical.

Of the many possible styles available – roller blinds, pleated Roman blinds, simple gathered festoon or Austrian blinds, paper blinds, and vertical louvres – one of the most flexible is the timeless venetian design that can cover the window completely, admit varying degrees of light as the angle of the slats is adjusted, or pull completely clear of the glass to flood the room with sun.

Like curtains, blinds can alter the apparent size and shape of a window; order one slightly wider than a too-narrow window to make it look squarer, or visually lengthen a disproportionately short one by hanging a blind above it, then making sure when you draw the blind up that its hem reaches only as far as the top of the frame.

ABOVE If you're lucky enough to have beautifully-shaped windows that provide plenty of light, are not overlooked, and offer outstanding views, you might be well advised to leave them completely unadorned. In this low, modern, California bedroom, nothing has been allowed to come between the natural earth colours of the rugs and textiles, and the stunning woodland vista outside. On a practical note, a simple, tailored cover, matching bolster, and piles of throw cushions have transformed a simple brass bedstead into an attractive and inviting daytime sofa.

SHUTTERS page 138

Curtains

Make sure all curtains or drapes admit the maximum amount of light by extending the rail or track on either side of the frame so they clear the glass completely when they're not in use. As a bonus, this arrangement can make a meagre-sized window look more generously proportioned. Get the most from windows set in the corner of a room, or awkwardly placed near a staircase, by hanging a double-width curtain that pulls to one side only. Tiny dormer windows do not usually have even the narrowest space beside them for curtain clearance, yet the illumination they provide is often desperately needed. If their construction prevents you from installing a blind instead, hang a plain, single curtain from a rail hinged at one end to swing out like a tea-towel holder.

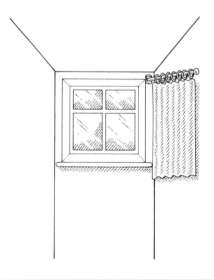

ABOVE *At a tiny, recessed window, fit shutters made from slim panels that can be folded away to let in as much light as possible.*

LEFT *For the same reason, make sure curtains can pull clear of the glass (or fix tie-backs). Extending the track on either side of the window will also make it look wider; if it's too short, attach a deep valance above it, so the bottom of the valance falls slightly below the top of the window.*

When it's a struggle to find room for the practical paraphernalia of everyday life, plants and flowers often come low on the list of space priorities, yet even the most enthusiastic inhabitants of a cramped urban environment seem to be cheered by the presence of growing things. Make room for them by using a little imagination.

Take advantage of the most obvious light source by suspending a row of plants from a curtain rail, screwed into the ceiling a little away from a window so it allows the curtains or blind to operate freely.

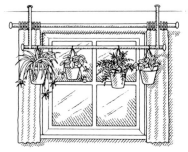

Hang several (in unusual baskets maybe, or an old-fashioned glass pendant lampshade) from shelf brackets fixed in the same position, or line a deep reveal with small pots of herbs sitting on tiny shelves or dangling from hooks or miniature brackets.

Extremely proficient DIY practitioners (or obsessive gardeners who are prepared to lay out a fairly hefty sum for a professional builder) could consider removing an

ordinary window altogether and replacing it with a scaled-down but authentic conservatory structure with an angled glass roof and a solid base cantilevered out from the original opening. Again, you would

have to sacrifice some light, but you would gain an impressive and ideal display area for plants.

Exploit dead space at high levels by lining a row of pretty specimens along the top of a wardrobe or a run of wall cupboards in the kitchen; add colour here by standing (or hanging) them in large tin cans with their cheerful labels still in place. Like bathrooms, kitchens are often perfect indoor-garden areas because of their high degree of humidity.

Make your plants earn their space by using a wall of them instead of a bulky piece of furniture to define separate areas of activity. For maximum effect, stand a row of tall ones on the floor, then suspend hanging varieties from the ceiling directly overhead.

The important thing to remember is that small, single plants dotted here and there in a hardworking room are almost bound to be lost completely. They will look much more attractive – and seem to thrive more consistently – in exotic clusters (perhaps on the floor, making a tiny indoor patio) or even in small groups of three or four.

LEFT *When your view is less than breathtaking, replace a conventional window treatment with a leafy plant. If you don't mind blocking out the sun, you could even fix a trellis over the whole window, inside or out, and put in a fast-growing species that filters light appealingly. To enlarge a too-shallow window sill, screw a deeper piece of wood on top of it, extending into the room. Alternatively, fix strong glass shelves across the window (making sure they're removable for cleaning) to hold rows of potted herbs or cuttings in a kitchen or living room.*

RIGHT *Take advantage of the kitchen's warmth and humidity by adorning any spare patch of wall with plant-filled shelves.*

Mirror dissolves the surface to which it is attached, extending space indefinitely, and it reflects light – both attributes that make it invaluable to small-space dwellers. Since mirror is available in sheets, tiles and tiny cloth-backed squares as well as in frames of varying size, shape and style, it is versatile enough for all sorts of situations.

Large expanses

A continuous covering of mirror over an entire surface is the most effective space-enhancer. Used on an entire wall, mirror visually doubles the room it reflects. At the end of a hall or passage, it makes the space appear endless; in an alcove, perhaps behind shelves, it gives the impression of a room beyond.

The cheapest and easiest way to cover any large area is with mirror tiles, and these are sold with an adhesive backing that makes them fairly straightforward to install. Unless your wall is perfectly flat however – and there are very few plaster walls without lumps and bumps – you should first put up a sheet of ply or chipboard on which to fix them, since even the slightest irregularity in the underlying surface will result in a badly distorted image. In a kitchen or bathroom, avoid using a porous material for backing, since it will absorb moisture that results in mould and causes damage to the silvering.

Alternatively, a single sheet of mirror will give a large, unbroken area of reflection, but it will certainly be more expensive to buy than tiles, and carry a far higher risk of breakage, as well as posing greater problems in installation. If you have the cash and the *sang-froid* to take on such a job however, be sure to choose a high-quality glass of sufficient thickness.

A wall of mirror is particularly well suited to spare, modern schemes, and will look even more dramatic if you make sure the view reflected is an attractive one – a beautiful window or an unusual piece of furniture, for example. Try to add interest at different levels by suspending a group of plants or a striking light fitting from the ceiling nearby, or by placing a carefully chosen picture or display of photographs on the opposite wall.

However impressive the effect, don't be tempted to increase it by treating facing walls this way, or you'll end up with a bizarre hall-of-mirrors effect that will drive you mad. Consider carefully before you install a huge sheet of mirror glass in an area used regularly for eating or relaxing, since even the least self-conscious individuals will find it disconcerting to catch sight of themselves constantly in mid-phrase or mid-mouthful. Similarly, think twice before you cover a whole wall with mirror in the bathroom, traditionally the smallest room and theoretically the one most in need of visual assistance. You might find it preferable to live with modest dimensions rather than to face your own reflection as you use the toilet or step naked and dripping from the bath. If however, because of the room's layout, this would not be a problem (or if you are without such vanity), fill the wall above the basin with mirror in sheet or tile form. As well as making the space seem bigger and brighter, it will accommodate family members of widely varying heights who shave or make up here.

Small reflections

If you find huge expanses of mirror overpowering, or if your home is more traditional in style, there are countless ways to make skilful use of smaller areas of reflection.

Because most people would like more light as well as more space in their homes, mirrors are particularly effective positioned near or around a window. Try using tiles

LEFT *Replace the standard doors on a run of fitted cupboards with sliding mirrored ones that brighten the room by reflecting natural and artificial light, provide a full-length view for dressing and grooming, and take up very little floor area in operation.*

RIGHT *For an even more dramatic effect, cover a whole wall with sheet mirror, making the room look twice its size. Here, the traditional girandole design (where a candle holder is attached to the front of a hanging mirror), has been enlarged and updated by fixing two shiny chrome wall lights directly onto the mirrored surface.*

ABOVE *Small sections of mirror can be used in a subtle way to expand space – this narrow hall seems to extend into the area taken up by the low* cupboards. *To get a similar effect, fix a narrow strip around a small room at skirting or cornice level, or along the front of shelves.*

or specially cut sheet mirror to cover the reveals completely; the deeper the window, the larger it will look and the more light it will appear to admit. On a bigger scale,

treat the walls on either side of a deeply-recessed window (such as those above a window seat) in the same way. In a small room with only a single window, hang next to it, or immediately facing it, a mirror of the same size and with a similar frame, to look like its pair. Where

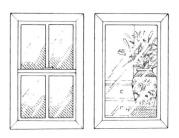

you want to conceal an unattractive view or ensure privacy (in a bathroom for example), replace the lower pane in a sash window with mirror glass. As a bonus, this will provide a grooming area that has the benefit of natural light.

Hang framed mirrors (old or new, ready-made or put together yourself) in places where you would normally display a picture: over a sofa, a table or a chest of drawers. A well-chosen collection of them grouped together looks particularly spectacular. In a child's room, choose a plain round mirror and construct a simple frame for it in the style of a port-hole. Again, wherever you put a mirror, make sure the view – both close-up and long-range – is worth reflecting. A selection of plants or a jug of flowers just in front of it looks twice as appealing, and a cluster of candles creates an enchanting glow.

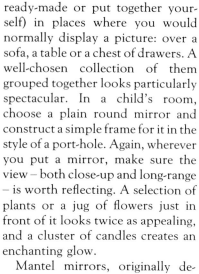

Mantel mirrors, originally designed to complement a decorative fireplace, can add drama and illumination to your home in a wide variety of locations. Some of the

most common sizes will fit a single or small double bed exactly to make a striking bedhead, but you should ensure that any large mirror in this position is completely secure to prevent it from toppling over in the night and causing serious injury. It's

best to play absolutely safe and screw it firmly to the wall.

For an unobtrusive touch of light and space in a dark corner, display a collection of decorative table-top mirrors, or insert mirror glass into one or more elegant, desk-top picture frames.

ABOVE A huge slab of mirror has worked its magic on this dark, miniscule internal bathroom. As well as performing its expected tasks of stretching space and enhancing light, it multiplies a striking collection of pictures, and serves the grooming needs of the tallest and shortest guests. Since this room has to cater for only one person, the shelf running all around it has been used for display, but it could also hold family toiletries.

RIGHT Prettily framed mantel mirrors have been in fashion for centuries, and old ones are still fairly easy to find. There are also many excellent reproduction designs available, or you could make a modern one from lengths of moulding.

Successful and well-planned lighting will fully illuminate all areas of activity and traffic paths, but in addition it will establish moods, define spaces and draw attention to – or disguise – each room's best – or worst – features. Never choose fittings purely on the basis of their appearance, but for what they contribute positively to a room's efficiency and atmosphere.

Avoid having a single pendant in the middle of the ceiling: it gives a harsh glare that is unflattering to the prettiest room and it does not provide the direct source of brightness you need for close work. Instead, use an assortment of small, well-placed lamps to establish and cater for areas of different (but possibly simultaneous) activity within a room, to highlight unusual details like cornices or pediments, or to show off an eye-catching display or treasured piece of furniture.

First establish where light is needed for practical purposes. At a desk or hobby area, try fixing a clamp light to a nearby shelf to keep the work surface clear, or choose a wall-mounted design. If you have room for only a small bedside table, fit your reading light in a similar position. You could even do away with table lamps by opting for wall or clamp versions instead; although clamp fittings have the disadvantage of a visible flex or cord, they allow you much greater flexibility than wall-fixed ones in the potential rearrangement of furniture.

Improve the apparent size of a room dramatically by moving several pieces of furniture away from the walls a little and placing uplighters behind them to soften the room's edges and blur their definition. In the same way, you can lift a low ceiling by 'painting' it with a soft glow, or try keeping all the lights at a low level if the room is disproportionately high.

To get an idea of the huge range of possible effects, take several small, portable lamps into your room when it's dark, and experiment with them in different positions and at various heights. Even without moving them around at all, you'll find that you can change the look of the room completely just by illuminating different combinations of them alternately.

One of the quickest, easiest and cheapest ways to add variety to a small room is by fitting a dimmer switch, which adapts the room's brightness instantly so it is perfectly suitable for serious studying at one moment, and a romantic dinner for two the next.

ABOVE *Try to provide a strong, direct source of illumination for long periods of paper work – the room's general lighting will not do. In this well-planned New York study, a pair of matching anglepoise fittings fulfils this function, and the pools of light they cast also effectively define the room's two separate work areas.*

RIGHT *The ceiling light in a pint-sized, Art Deco bedroom is ingeniously surrounded by inset mirrors to multiply its effect and make the space look higher. Above the platform, wall lights act as bedside illumination. During waking hours, attention is drawn lower by lighting only the spot in the tiny display area.*

It would be difficult to guess that this light, stylish flat is the basement of an old house, since the couple who live here have overcome the usual problems of living in small dark rooms by employing an impressive armoury of decorating skills and tactics. To achieve the cool, clean feeling they wanted, they first banished all fabrics and carpets, then limited the colour scheme throughout to white and black, with touches of red for accent. Even the two resident cats are black and white respectively, but their owners claim this is coincidence.

BELOW *Like the rest of the flat, the living room has a floor of square white quarry tiles. To make it look larger, these have been extended to cover the low seating/display platform, which conceals an extra storage area underneath. A huge glass coffee table in the middle of the room takes up no* visual space at all, and at night, light from the tall sleek standard lamp seems to lift the ceiling.

RIGHT *The entrance hall features three more examples of decorative detailing used throughout the flat: fine black venetian blinds, crisp black skirting (baseboard) and slim red radiators. Even the picture collection and the vase of flowers carry through the colour theme.*

FAR RIGHT *Alongside the flat, an extension built on to the original house had left a long, narrow walled courtyard. By adding a fourth wall and a pitched glass roof to let in the clear northern light, this was turned into a studio from which one of the occupants operates a small design consultancy. Warmth is provided by an underfloor system through the slim black grill running down the centre. Since the door at the end leads to an extra bathroom, its glass panels were replaced with pieces of mirror to give a similar effect.*

ABOVE LEFT *Where the hall widens, there is just room for a dining table that seats six; cantilevered chairs have been chosen (like those in the living room) for the lightness of their frame. Signature touches of red can be found in the rise and fall lamp and the cupboard and door handles.*

LEFT *In the kitchen, smaller white tiles have been extended up the walls, over a box structure that houses the extractor unit and the recessed*

lighting, and even across the ceiling. Side by side, a separate refrigerator and freezer can tuck under the cook-top, since the oven is wall mounted at a convenient height nearby.

ABOVE *In order that as little visual space as possible was lost, all the high-level cupboards were removed from the kitchen, and replaced with see-through wire mesh shelves; clear glass storage jars, chosen for the same reason, make their contents easy to identify .*

ABOVE *Separating the bath from the basin area, a slim, tiled partition wall takes the place of a shower curtain, and provides a surface on which to fix a row of glass shelves.*

RIGHT *The wall of bookshelves behind the bed is also false; it conceals a deep walk-in cupboard that extends along one whole side of the room. The mattress has been set into a low platform, tiled, like the one in the living room, so it appears to be an extension of the floor.*

USING SPACE ROOM BY ROOM

Every room presents its own challenges to the small-space dweller. In some, you may be able to solve problems simply with careful planning and organization; in others, it's a matter of choosing compact and space-saving versions of necessary furnishings and fittings. The most useful tactics will adapt to many situations, so keep an open mind and investigate even the topics that seem irrelevant.

MAKING PLANS

Any room will give greater satisfaction if the arrangement of its furniture and accessories is well thought out. It's not enough just to run through in your mind the possible positions of each furnishing item; you should measure every room carefully with a metal rule (fabric ones stretch) and draw an accurate scale plan of it on a large sheet of paper. (Graph paper will make the job easier.) Then, measure and mark out the doors, showing the 90cm (3ft) clearance needed for any that open into the room. Do the same for the windows, noting the height of each from the floor so you can judge which items can go under it. Add to your floor plan electrical outlets and switches, wall lights, telephone socket, radiators and anything else that is fixed. Note down as well any predetermined traffic paths – like between two doors or a door and a large window.

Now cut out to the same scale outlines of every item of furnishing that will take up floor space; peripatetic room-planners should use heavy card or even balsa wood so these models can be kept, and this process doesn't have to be repeated every time they move. Dealing with major pieces first, move these cut-outs around on your plan to get an idea of potential locations for each. Since the size of the room will probably impose heavy restrictions on the number of arrangements possible, don't add to your problems by insisting that all

PAGE 44 *Take advantage of a deeply recessed window by fitting built-in seating. Here, a simple fabric-covered platform supports mounds of plump cushions.*

ABOVE *A compact kitchen can work more efficiently than a huge one, since everything is close at hand. For convenience and safety, make sure there is somewhere to put things down* next to the sink, the cook-top, the oven and the refrigerator.

RIGHT *A large room that has to fulfil many functions poses just as many problems as a small one. Inspired planning and a sure sense of style have enabled this long, narrow space to serve as kitchen, dining room, bedroom and living room – and look extraordinarily inviting at the same time.*

the furniture be lined up against the walls like a waiting room. Placing a large item in the middle of the floor could give you much more flexibility; a long, narrow living room, for example, will seem a much more pleasing shape if the sofa is set at right angles to a long wall rather than along its length.

You should leave clear traffic paths at least 60cm (2ft) wide between the door and any large or often-used items: television, bed, etc., making sure that no traffic is directed through a conversation area. Your furniture should look inviting to use and easy to get to.

Once you've worked out the optimum position for your existing pieces, you will be able to identify gaps in your furnishing arrangements and establish the maximum possible size of the items you need to fill them. Check every dimension twice and be sure to measure between two walls not only at floor level, but further up the walls as well in case they are more than slightly uneven. This meticulous care is particularly necessary when the article in question has been ordered specially for you and is therefore unreturnable.

The other measurements that it's essential to get right are those that involve the access of any bulky piece of furniture; check out not only the door of the relevant room, but also any landing, staircase and main entrance it will have to pass through on its way.

LIVING ROOMS

In most modern households, the living room has taken over from the kitchen as the hub of the home and the place around which most of the activities are centred. In addition to providing the main area for relaxing and entertaining, it is often forced into service as a dining room, guest room, study and music room as well. If this is your problem, first investigate the possibility of diverting one or two extra functions to other locations. Could one of the bedrooms double as a study, or house the television or stereo? Maybe a wide hall or landing, equipped with a folding or flap-down table, would serve as a work or dining area.

Next, look carefully at the components of your living room; a small space that works as hard as this one cannot afford to carry any furnishing item that doesn't pull its weight, so everything in it must be hardwearing, easy to look after and suitable for its purpose; reject exquisite but uncomfortable chairs, tables with a surface too delicate to put anything on, or white carpet that would be ruined by one cup of spilled coffee.

To avoid disasters like this, and to make the room as convenient in use as possible, try to be sure that every seat has a table surface of some kind near it so plates, cups and glasses don't have to be balanced precariously on knees or set down on the floor where they're likely to be kicked over. Similarly,

ABOVE *An L-shaped banquette makes the best possible use of space in a tiny townhouse. Built-in seating also offers extra storage capacity if you provide access to the base.*

RIGHT *To keep a hardworking room looking its best, choose furnishing materials that will stand up to constant wear, in colours and patterns that don't show every mark.*

if your living room accommodates an eating area, be sure the table is located near the door, so setting and clearing can be done as quickly, easily and safely as possible.

Seating

No matter how many extraneous functions your living room fulfils, it's primarily a place where family and friends can relax, so sorting out your seating arrangements should be your number one priority.

For the main seating, invest in at least one or two properly upholstered pieces, since smaller, cheaper and less formal sofas and chairs will never give you the same comfort and support. Reject the tyranny of the three-seat sofa in favour of the much more useful and flexible two-seater design: the larger version is seldom used by more than two in any case, as most people like the security of a corner and the comfort of an arm. Choose loose covers (slipcovers) rather than fixed ones so you can remove them easily for cleaning. You could even invest in two sets of covers to provide a fresh look for your room from time to time. Buy (or cover) a pouffe (or ottoman) to match, and you'll have an extra seat that can be moved around as needed, and a useful temporary dumping place for magazines and newspapers.

A great deal of flexibility can often be gained by the use of unit (sectional) seating, which you can buy in corner or side pieces and

assemble in a suitable way for your space and your needs; make a large L-shaped arrangement that lines one wall and comes out at right angles into the room for example, or go for two or three chairs or small sofas with components that can be moved around to suit your changing requirements.

Both unit seating and ordinary ranges of upholstery are often available with scaled-down proportions specially for small rooms; the tiniest space gain might affect your seating possibilities dramatically, so it's worth asking around. Enquire too whether your chosen design comes in sofa-bed form so you can put up occasional overnight guests in comfort.

If you are prepared to trade off maximum use of space for flexibility in arrangement, install built-in seating, maybe in a U-shaped configuration at one end of a small room. If the seats are deep enough, one of them would serve as a bed for visitors.

Employ visual trickery by placing a built-in sofa (or a freestanding one) on a recessed base so it appears to float in space, giving the impression of a much larger floor area.

When it comes to positioning your furniture, you must make sure each seat has clear access and enough space around it for safe, convenient use. Sofas and chairs need 45 cm (1ft 6in) legroom in front; if they are in the middle of a room, they should have 60cm (2ft)

LEFT *Take full advantage of a deep window recess by installing a low platform covered with squab and throw cushions to give extra seating capacity. Here again, the space underneath has been given over to storage by fitting sliding doors.*

ABOVE *A two-seater sofa offers much more flexibility in the room's arrangement than a larger version, which will often fit in only one position. Similarly, two small coffee tables can be used separately when you fancy a change or for entertaining. Note the subtle visual trick of painting the skirting (baseboard) to match the floor, making it look much larger.*

RIGHT *Turn the area above your sofa into a mini-library by filling it with narrow shelves, making sure the bottom one is high enough to allow plenty of headroom. For support, use decorative brackets that are stout enough, and spaced sufficiently close together, to prevent collapse. To make the structure less obtrusive, colour shelves and brackets to match the wall behind them.*

between their backs and the nearest wall or item of furniture to allow traffic to pass. For easy conversation, seating should be arranged so people are at right angles to, or facing, each other, not in a straight line like a bus queue.

Supplementary seats   Once you have fulfilled your main seating requirements, there are many ways you can expand these facilities for occasional larger-scale entertaining. Invest in stacking chairs or folding ones that can be hung up or tucked away in a cupboard when they are not required; fabric-covered deck and directors' chairs are much more comfortable than rigid ones and can be made up in a wide range of materials – be bold and display

them on the walls of a modern room as part of the decoration, in the Shaker style.

Cover several large, thick squares of foam in washable fabric and stack them neatly so they don't take up much room. Bring them out when you need additional seating, or lay them side by side to provide temporary sleeping accommodation.

If you have a bay or bow window, build a roomy window seat underneath and add a generous fitted pad, plus a large assortment of cushions. For valuable extra storage space, hinge the lid, or fit cupboard doors in the front.

A slim, backless bench makes a space-saving coffee table and will do double duty as extra seating that is easy to move around.

LEFT *Keep a few floor cushions stacked away to cater for unexpected guests. In this cool corner, a low-level cupboard has been rendered almost invisible by lifting it off the floor and painting it white to blend with the rest of the scheme.*

RIGHT *Squeezed between two large windows, a slim floor-to-ceiling shelf unit stores a large number of magazines and tall books in a space that is usually wasted.*

Storage

Consider how extra capacity might be squeezed out of furniture meant for other purposes. Apart from exploiting the space under built-in seating, you can find many useful storage pieces that will also serve as tables; small chests of drawers, for instance, might be just the right height for side tables, while any large, flat-topped wooden or metal chest, trunk or blanket box would make an ideal coffee table. If you

have room, look for a designers' plan chest to fill this function – these contain several shallow but huge drawers that would swallow up no end of household clutter. Even if you can't combine every occasional table with a fully fledged piece of storage furniture, at least select one with a shelf underneath.

For the room's main storage, you can choose either freestanding units or some kind of built-in system, according to your needs, your taste,

Designer: John Wright

your budget and the length of time you intend to stay in your present home. Fitted storage undoubtedly makes the best use of available space, and in its simplest form – open shelving – it is not expensive to construct, but it cannot be moved around easily and must be abandoned or dismantled when you move. Give fitted shelves as much flexibility as possible by making them adjustable in height to allow for items of different sizes, or leave one shelf fixed and fit two or three drawers under it to provide a catch-all for small odds and ends.

Purpose-built storage units on the other hand, can be shifted from place to place fairly easily and taken with you to your next home, but they tend to be costly, and what's more important, you're unlikely to find one that fits your chosen space exactly. A unit like this might be very useful however, to divide a larger area into separate spheres of activity: living and dining, or even living and cooking.

RIGHT *Industrial shelving components have been bolted together to make a visually weightless storage unit for domestic electronic equipment. Unsightly accessories like headphones and tools for cleaning and repair are stored in wicker hampers.*

One good solution to the fitted vs-freestanding dilemma might be a range of the wooden or plastic cube storage units mentioned earlier, which are extremely strong and come with shelves, drawers, doors, etc.. You can build up your collection of these as your requirements and your cashflow situation allow, then shift them from one location to another – a big plus for those in rented accommodation.

Sound ideas One of the biggest storage headaches in modern living rooms is the relentless proliferation of electronic equipment: television, video, tape recorder and stereo or CD player. To prevent them from looking like a motley assortment of boxes trailing endless wires and flexes, collect your home entertainment equipment into a single unit or piece of furniture. If you don't use these items every day, or if your room is traditional in design, concealing them behind doors will look neat and uncluttered, as well as protecting your expensive toys from dust. If they are in frequent use however, a run of doors left constantly open will only add to the impression of untidiness, so it would be best to keep everything accessible.

Before you build shelves or select items of special storage furniture, measure each piece of equipment carefully, then check its wiring arrangements and the way in which it's used to see if any extra space is needed; some wires project from the back at right angles to protect the connection for example, and many stereo turntables are covered with plastic flip-top lids that take up considerable room in operation.

If open storage is your choice, neaten cords and flexes by gathering them loosely together with wire bag closures or masking tape. Even in the most restricted space, never display plants or flowers nearby, since even a few drops of water on a piece of electrical equipment could be damaging and dangerous.

Those who want to hide all their high-tech gear away should have no trouble finding a suitable storage unit, but it's also possible to make use of an existing piece of furniture, perhaps one that fits into a traditional scheme. In addition to ensuring that every item fits inside your dresser (hutch) or cupboard, including knobs and switches, you will have to provide adequate ventilation and access for wiring. Try to avoid drilling holes in a valuable

RIGHT *Vary the depth of shelves in a storage system so they can accommodate items of different sizes without wasting any space. The large amount of light that pours into this New York apartment makes the dramatic all-black scheme workable.*

piece of furniture; remove one or two boards instead, or take off the back entirely and keep it in case you ever want to return the piece to its original state.

Whether your main pieces of sound equipment are concealed or displayed, you will have to find room for a pair – or even a quartet – of bulky speakers. Rather than using up valuable floor or shelf space, fix them on the wall with discreet but sturdy brackets.

Tables

In many small homes, one large table in the living room provides the only place where a multitude of activities – eating, studying, playing games, pursuing hobbies, paying bills, etc – can be carried on, so it's vital that you choose the right one. It must be stable and strong, with a surface that takes spills, scratches and knocks. Your table should be not only large enough to cope with the demands made on it, but the most comfortable height for you and your family and the right shape

to make the best possible use of its allotted space; a round table for example will tuck neatly into a corner of a square room, while a rectangular table would be the wisest choice for one end of a long narrow area. If a large rectangular table would best suit your needs and your space, invest in two small square ones instead; they could be pushed together for formal meals, then separated after dinner to be used in different parts of the room.

If you eat elsewhere, try to provide at least one desk-height table or work surface in the living room for general use, preferably one with drawers so the surface can be kept clear.

Those who entertain regularly could consider acquiring a set of nesting tables, which are useful for drinks, snacks and casual meals, yet they tuck away neatly when they are no longer required. Since they're light to carry, you can also move one or all of them to any other room where extra surfaces are needed temporarily.

LEFT *Instead of blocking up a chimney breast, exploit the area inside by replacing the fireplace with small cupboards and drawers. Here, the alcoves on either side have been filled to capacity, yet the bottom shelf clears the floor to avoid reducing the apparent size of the room.*

RIGHT *Large expanses of fitted shelves have been absorbed into a faithfully recreated Art Deco scheme by keeping them simple. and eschewing sharp corners in favour of curves, in the style of the period. Extra-deep shelves will hold cards and display objects as well as books.*

KITCHENS

Although more hard work – and more diverse and complex work – is probably carried on in the kitchen than anywhere else in the home, architects and builders often relegate this room to postage-stamp size as their first line of attack against space problems. You can cope with such inadequacy only by drawing up your own battle plan based around the way you shop for, prepare, cook and serve your meals.

How many people do you cook for? How often do you cook? How often do you shop? How often do you entertain? Once you get a clear idea of what you need from your kitchen, you can begin to help it to fulfil those needs. Say for example, you work full time and prepare only a simple meal for one or two in the evening, yet you can't get to the shops more than once every few weeks. You will need a large fridge/freezer and lots of food storage facilities, but you could get by with less space for dishes and equipment, and a smaller preparation area. If, however, you are at home, cooking three elaborate meals a day for a family, you will need the maximum possible working space and plenty of room for crockery, saucepans and utensils, but you may be able to shop frequently, so large-scale food storage will be less important.

When you are equipping your kitchen from scratch, buy the best quality fittings you can afford. The more restricted your space, the more wear everything in it will get – not

only floors and countertops, but cupboard hinges and drawer handles will be in constant use. While planning where each item will go, remember that an unbroken stretch of working surface is more convenient and flexible than two or three smaller, separate sections. In a very tiny kitchen area, you may even be able to exploit extra space in a tight corner by staggering the depth of the counter slightly.

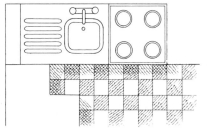

If possible, choose wall-hung units rather than floor-standing ones, since they give the illusion of greater space, they make floor cleaning much easier, and they can be fixed at the most convenient height for the cook. In addition, wall-hung units neatly avoid the fixing problems caused by an uneven floor.

LEFT *Choose fitted storage units that come in a wide range of shapes and sizes, so you can fill every bit of available space with cupboards, drawers and shelves.*

When you're deciding where to position cupboards (and shelves) and what to put in each one – or if you're stuck with your existing set-up – keep in mind the huge difference you can make to the efficiency of your kitchen simply by storing every item near where it is most often used. Similarly, make sure that all items in everyday use are stored between shoulder and hip height so you aren't constantly bending and stretching. For this reason too, fix wall cupboards 40–45cm (16–18in) above base units so they are within easy reach, yet leave enough space above the work surface for small appliances in use.

Give an impression of continuity to the room by choosing quarry or heavy-duty ceramic tiles for the floor, and carry them over the worktop and up the wall to form a splashback. When it comes to decoration, avoid large expanses of pattern and ornamentation; keep everything simple and let the shapes and colours of your equipment and the bright packaging of your groceries provide visual interest.

ABOVE *An unbroken sweep of terracotta tiles – on the floor, over the counter, and up the wall – pulls together this small, awkwardly-shaped kitchen, and provides a hardwearing, easy-to-clean surface.*

Storage

Although kitchens – like all other living spaces – appear to get smaller and smaller, storage requirements in this room have increased dramatically in the last few decades. Not only do we seem to need a huge assortment of tools and appliances, but we now have access to a large range of general and specialist food-stuffs that our parents' generation never even heard of.

Try initially to reduce this burden by choosing your tableware and cooking equipment wisely: there is no room in a mini kitchen for a collection of odd plates, bowls and cups that seldom get used, or for additional, 'best', sets of china, glass and cutlery, so look for one well-designed range of each that can be dressed up or down to suit any occasion. Invest in baking dishes that can be used for serving and freezing as well, and buy a few really sharp knives that will do lots of different jobs. Make space in your drawers by getting rid of under-employed gadgets – when did you last need a cherry stoner?

If you entertain infrequently, keep only the tableware you use for everyday meals in the kitchen, storing back-up supplies elsewhere.

Your kitchen will never function efficiently if the work surface is constantly cluttered, so fit a shelf above it to hold small appliances when they're not needed, and screw hooks underneath for your mugs.

FAR LEFT *Too often, much needed low-level storage space is taken up with a forest of pipes, but you can prevent this by running all plumbing under the base units (if they are wall-mounted) or inside their plinths (if they sit on the floor). Alternatively, bring the units forward a little so the plumbing can be fixed behind, but extend the work surface right back to the wall to conceal it. Make sure there is still at least 125cm (3ft 6in) clearance however, so you can bend to open a cupboard, and so someone can pass behind you as you work. Here, a slim counter fixed at right angles provides a place to eat breakfast and quick snacks, relieving pressure on the main dining area. A small pull-out table (plus stacking stools) would do the same job.*

LEFT *A narrow shelf just above the work surface holds the small bottles and boxes you're forever losing (or moving out of the way) in a large cupboard. On this carefully thought-out storage wall, the shelves are positioned close enough together so no space is wasted.*

RIGHT *To get the most from a high-level storage area, fix a wide mesh shelf to hold bulky, seldom-used articles, then hang everyday utensils (even herbs) from butcher's hooks underneath so they're within easy reach. Or just suspend a length of dowelling above the cook-top to hold pots and spoons.*

This area above the counter is the most accessible in the room so fill any leftover space with a cutlery or knife rack, a spoon box, a wall-hung handmixer or set of scales, or a low, very narrow shelf for small tins, packets and bottles. Fit a wall-mounted tooth-mug holder and soap dish from a bathroom range for liquid detergent and scouring pads, and position your draining rack over the sink rather than beside it; everyday dishes can live here permanently.

Clear as many things as possible out of the cupboards and drawers and off the floor on to the walls, by fixing a row of hooks, a sheet of pegboard, or a wooden or wire grid on which to suspend saucepans, utensils, ovengloves and tea towels, mugs, baskets and even, *in extremis*, string bags full of fruit and vegetables, cleaning materials or bulky

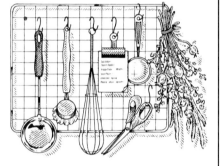

tins and packets. If there is only a small patch of wall available, a cooling rack would do the same job on a small scale. You could even cover a window that doesn't provide a great deal of light or an attractive view with a similar grid system or a row of shelves, and treat the back of the kitchen door the same way, fixing a small lip to any shelves to prevent your things from falling out when the door is in use.

Fix a wide shelf just below ceiling level to hold large, seldom-used pieces of equipment. Consider replacing some or all of your high-level cupboards with open shelves to make the room look larger and less closed in, or at least remove the

LEFT *If tins and packets continually get lost in the murky reaches of a deep, narrow cupboard, replace this with pull-out larder shelves, whose contents are always kept neat and easy to see.*

ABOVE The artist-owner of this extraordinary kitchen has accommodated his extensive collections of tins, china, cooking equipment and food (real and fake) by fitting out the room with freestanding and fitted units to resemble an old-fashioned shop, where sound planning was just as necessary as it is in a modern home.

RIGHT Show off a collection of pretty glasses by displaying them on open shelves made of the same material, so light can pass through freely. Delicate, unobtrusive brass brackets give plenty of support over such a narrow span.

doors and add blinds or simple washable curtains instead that take up far less room.

No matter how big they are, most cupboards have only a single shelf inside, which means that tins and boxes – and much more dangerously, china and glass – have to be piled high to avoid wasting huge amounts of valuable space. Overcome this problem by screwing hooks along the top and under the shelf, or fixing a hanging rack for stemmed glasses. Add extra shelves in between the existing ones, clip a wire basket to the underside of the central shelf, or fix one that slides out on runners to hold tea towels or

Where at all possible, try to squeeze in one tall cupboard so you can hide away unlovely necessities like the ironing board, vacuum cleaner, broom, mop etc.

Those who dislike fitted kitchens – or those unwilling or unable to install them – could adapt storage furniture designed for other purposes. Resurrect an old wardrobe for instance, by painting it to match the walls so it 'disappears'. Fit it out with shelves and hooks and you'll

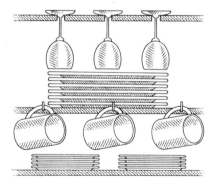

paper napkins. Line very deep cupboards with pull-out shelves or baskets and deal with corner models by installing a carousel unit or Lazy Susan so you can see immediately what's at the back. Find a place to fix vertical dividers so you have somewhere to keep your chopping boards, tart tins and trays, both serving and baking.

ABOVE *Exploit the otherwise dead space between shelves by installing a tiny, top-fixed hanging rail to hold cups and mugs – or simply screw in one or two rows of hooks.*

ABOVE *Many small storage fittings, like knife racks, kitchen-paper holders and baskets (wire or wicker), can be attached to existing units as well as to the wall.*

RIGHT *Replace the space-consuming doors on your storage units with blinds or curtains, like the stylish and practical chain mail ones in this dramatic modern kitchen. Choosing a floor covering in the same silvery colour makes the room look bigger.*

LEFT *Available in several different sizes and depths, roomy wire storage baskets operate on top-fixed runners. A simpler version clips on to a shelf or work surface; since it does not pull out to give access from the top, this type is open at the front.*

ABOVE *When there is almost no counter or cupboard space, all the room's storage capacity has to be provided by the walls. Tongue and groove cladding is easy to fix into, gives an illusion of height, and hides bumps and cracks.*

have masses of space for food, china, glass and linen. Make use of a roomy chest of drawers, and paint an old bookcase to provide lots of open shelving. One of the most useful items of freestanding kitchen furniture is the old-fashioned cabinet with glass doors at the top, a flap-down work surface and cupboards underneath. These can usually be bought very cheaply indeed and transformed by fixing new glass or gathered curtains in the doors, replacing the handles and adding a fresh coat of paint. To store small items like spices, look for an old smoking chest or bathroom cabinet that can be hung on the wall.

A wooden or metal trolley (preferably one with shelves or even drawers) would furnish you with an additional work surface – maybe a special one like butcher's block or marble – as well as quite a lot of storage space. Tuck it away in a corner or under the counter, and wheel it to a convenient place when it's needed. (A trolley can be very useful in other rooms as well: to hold home office supplies in the living room for example, or sewing equipment in the bedroom.)

RIGHT *Many old windows were fitted with large shutters, and shallow recesses into which they folded away. If the shutters have been replaced with blinds or curtains, line the redundant space with narrow shelves for storage or display.*

Equipment

You're very lucky indeed if you have enough space – or enough money – for all the equipment and appliances you would like to own, so here again, you'll probably have to compromise. Some facilities – those for chilling, cooking and basic washing – you can't do without, but all others are optional. Small appliances take up valuable counter space and are bulky and inconvenient to store elsewhere, so don't allow yourself any that cannot justify their existence by constant use. In terms of large pieces of equipment, give first priority to those that perform the jobs you least enjoy. If you hate washing dishes more than you hate shopping, a dishwasher would be a wiser choice than a freezer; if going to the launderette is your idea of hell, but cooking doesn't inspire you much either, do without a full-sized cooker (range) to make room for a washer/drier, and perform culinary tasks with a slim cook-top and a small multi-purpose oven.

As well as traditional freestanding models, most major domestic appliances are available in a version specially designed to be built in. If you're planning your kitchen from scratch, choose these integrated appliances to give a co-ordinated, sleek look, but remember they're often expensive, and awkward to take with you when you move and, unlike freestanding ones, seldom available in scaled-down versions.

Try combining some of the smaller appliances in unusual ways; put a multi-purpose oven at eye level, over a small fridge, for example, or tuck it beneath a work surface, over a deep drawer.

Refrigerators and freezers While a refrigerator is indispensable, the usefulness of a freezer in a small kitchen will vary from person to person. Even when you are able to shop regularly, you may find it earns its keep if you have access to home-grown produce, if you prepare several meals at one time, or if you depend heavily on frozen, ready-prepared dishes.

Fridges and freezers, both separate and combined, are available in so many permutations (including very tiny ones meant for office and bar use) that you're bound to find something to suit your needs. Consider a particularly narrow upright fridge/freezer – they come with a bigger fridge than freezer or vice versa, and with either unit at the top – or go for same size, under-the-counter designs. Rather than opening in the normal way, some low-level refrigerators and freezers pull out, like a very deep drawer with stacked baskets inside, so access is from the top and you don't have to crouch or bend over to see what's inside. Check to see if the door of your appliance should be hinged on the right or the left for maximum convenience and the best possible use of space.

When there is no room for a separate freezer in the kitchen, maybe a small upright or chest model could be housed in a cupboard, cellar or garage. If you are really desperate, tuck an undersized one in a corner of the living or bedroom – as long as you allow for ventilation, you could even use a pretty cloth to disguise it.

Cooking facilities Like fridges and freezers, appliances that perform some kind of cooking function are sold in a huge variety of sizes and types. If you want the standard single appliance with the cook-top at waist level and the oven below, you can choose an integrated design (usually known as built-under), a completely freestanding model, or a slot-in type, which is a freestanding one specially made to fit flush with kitchen units. Again, integrated appliances are not usually available in extra small sizes, but you can often find a freestanding one slim enough to fit the tightest spot. Look for a ceramic cook-top or one with a toughened glass lid that closes over the rings when they are not in use, both of which provide an extra work surface.

These days, it has become increasingly popular to separate the cook-top from the oven completely, and, though more expensive, this approach solves many space problems as well as allowing two people to cook at the same time in a tiny kitchen. Install your oven

ABOVE *Freestanding appliances are available in small versions for use in tight corners, and you can take them with you easily when you move.*

RIGHT *In a galley kitchen, the separate cook-top has been accommodated in a shallow counter by choosing a design that features an ingenious arrangement of burners. Small appliances not in use are stored on a high-level shelf nearby so the work surface is kept clear.*

at eye level to save bending, or put it under a shallow counter, since it isn't as deep as a four-ring cook-top. Whether the oven is separate or part of a traditional cooker (range), consider a multi-function electric model that combines a microwave facility with a standard operation and a grill. If you already have an ordinary oven, and would like a microwave to supplement it, look for one of the extra-small models on the market – many can be wall mounted or fixed under a cupboard so they don't take up work space.

When it comes to the cook-top, position it over a cupboard or a deep appliance like a washer or dishwasher; some are so slim they can even go over the drawer where you keep your cooking utensils. Both gas and electric ones are available with two rings instead of four; use these when your cooking requirements are minimal, or to range four elements in a row across the back of a slightly deeper work surface, giving you an unbroken run of counter and providing an extra safety feature for any children in the home. As with combined appliances, choose a separate cook-top that offers extra counter space when it's not in use.

Those who have little interest in cooking, or too restricted a space for even the smallest oven and cook-top, could invest in a small table-top appliance consisting of a wee oven with a grill, and two rings on top, or a flat metal plate that can be used as an element or griddle.

Don't neglect the potential of minor pieces of equipment like a stacking steamer, which can cook a meal on one burner, or a double saucepan (double boiler).

Sinks and taps While there are some amazingly tiny sinks available, they are not very practical, since their capacity is inadequate for most people's dishwashing needs, and they can't cope with large items like oven shelves and roasting trays. It's not necessary to resort to these miniature models in any case, since many designs are available with chopping boards, draining racks, bowls and colanders that drop over them to provide extra work space. If you prepare a great deal of food, you'll find it useful to have two sinks, even if one of them is only half sized.

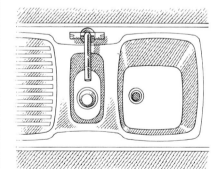

Again, you can justify the extra room it takes by adding one of the above accessories. It may be that the best use of your room can be made by siting the sink in a corner, and there are specially shaped ones for this purpose.

To clear the work space around your sink, plumb the taps into the wall behind it, or look for a neat, compact, single-block mixer tap.

Washers and driers It's worth making every possible effort to provide laundry facilities somewhere in your home, since few prospects are more depressing than ploughing regularly through a mountain of hand washing, or spending your free time in the launderette. There is no reason of course, why washing cannot be done elsewhere – when there is space, the bathroom is an ideal location, and if you can organize the plumbing satisfactorily, any spare cupboard or corner will do. In practice however, most washers and driers seem to end up in the kitchen.

To squeeze an automatic washer into a tiny space, either look for a scaled-down version of a standard front-loader, which takes a smaller load (but uses less water, detergent and energy as well) or choose a top-loading model, which can be up to 33 per cent narrower than a full-sized one, yet copes with a full load. Find a make that rolls out from under the counter, so you don't waste any worktop space.

Tumble driers are also available in miniature versions that line up beside a matching washer or stack

FAR LEFT *A double sink makes life easier for the busy cook; keep one full of soapy water to wash up as you go, and use the other for rinsing fruit and vegetables. Note the separate cook-top, which offers a choice of gas or electric burners.*

ABOVE *Plumb taps into the wall to keep the sink area completely clear, or to make room for a larger model. This tiny kitchen has a subtle strip of mirror along the front of the work-top to enlarge it visually.*

on top of it – some can even be hung on the wall. At a pinch, rig up an old-fashioned rise-and-fall clothes line that hoists up to the ceiling, then lowers when you want to remove dry articles, or fix a smaller telescopic one that pulls out to provide a row of lines over the bath.

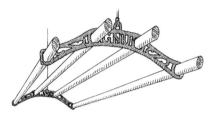

If you can manage one full-sized appliance, solve all your laundry problems by investing in a combination washer/drier. These have an advantage over a separate drier in that many need no ventilation – they come with their own condenser so moist air is converted into water and expelled through the waste pipe. A small disadvantage is that when a combined machine goes wrong, you lose both functions instead of just one. The drying capacity of all washer/driers is considerably less than the washing capacity, so you have to remove some of the load before putting the tumbler into operation.

One company manufactures a top-loading washer/drier that offers all the advantages of a front-loader, yet is 25 per cent narrower.

Dishwashers Simple sloth is not the only reason for a busy person

with a small kitchen to acquire a dishwasher; in a tiny space, where only a few dirty dishes look like a major mess, you'll welcome the opportunity of hiding away plates and pots as soon as they're finished with so the room looks pristine. Use the rinse facility after every meal, then put the machine through its full cycle only once a day or less.

Although dishwashers are available to cope with anything up to 14 place settings, there are several compact versions on the market that do an excellent job on crockery for four or six. The most efficient are restricted only in capacity – they have a full-sized motor. You can connect these mini-designs to the taps when needed, or plumb them in fully; they will sit on the worktop or draining board, or tuck underneath. Although dishwashers usually load from the front, it's also possible to find small top-loaders that pull out on runners from inside a cupboard.

Waste When you need space desperately, it's a great shame to squander any of it on storing accumulated rubbish, yet this is likely to happen when waste has to be carried a long distance away from your kitchen for collection. A waste disposal unit fitted under your sink will deal swiftly with organic material, but it's the bottles, tins and boxes that really mount up. In a space not much more than that taken up by a full-sized rubbish bin (garbage can)

ABOVE *Save steps by storing your plates and glasses near the dishwasher or sink. If wall space is tight, run the water supply to a peninsular unit, and fix suspended shelves overhead.*

RIGHT *Keep the kitchen clear of organic waste (and the resulting smells) by investing in a waste disposal unit that fits under the sink. Span wall units with a draining rack directly above it to keep the counter clear.*

you could install a compactor that squeezes a week's refuse for a family of four into a single neat bag, while neutralizing any odour.

Ventilation Even if you don't mind cooking smells permeating your small home, you should provide adequate ventilation in the kitchen to prevent condensation and grease build-up.

To cope with steam, smells, and grease from cooking, a cooker hood is the ideal choice, but this alone may not cope adequately with vapour from other appliances, like a non-vented tumble drier. A wall- or window-mounted extractor should deal with any problems however, as long as you choose an appropriate size for your room (ask your dealer for advice); try to position the cooking surface as near it as possible to minimize ducting.

You can help the situation greatly yourself by using a little common sense. Keep lids on saucepans and avoid rapid boiling; turn the kettle off as soon as it boils, or buy an automatic one; insulate a particularly cold wall to prevent condensation and don't fling the window open on a cold day.

Vacuum cleaners Single people living in bijou dwellings are unlikely to need a full-sized vacuum cleaner, which is bulky to store anyway, so they could settle for a small hand-operated one that is mains powered for maximum efficiency.

EATING PLACES

Whether you eat in a dining room, a kitchen, a living room, or an ingeniously carved-out niche elsewhere, you will want to make sure not only that meals can be served conveniently, but that family and friends are as comfortable as possible.

To this end, your table should be 75cm (2ft 6in) high with 30cm (12in) between the top and the chair seats for knees – more if diners like to cross their legs. Each place setting needs 37.5cm (15in) in depth, and 70cm (2ft 4in) in width for elbow room. Ideally, chair backs should be 40cm (16in) high for support. Leave a corridor of 90cm (3ft) between the table and the nearest wall or item of furniture so chairs can be moved in and out and people can pass behind – slightly more if the table is next to a surface from which food is served.

Look for a table that can be expanded: with a drop end, gate-leg fashion, or an inserted leaf. Choose a square or rectangular design to provide the maximum number of full-sized places, or a round one if you want to squeeze in as many as possible: a round table may also leave space for a small corner cupboard. A pedestal support will give the room a more spacious appearance and avoids table legs becoming entwined with those of the diners.

Even if they take up more room than standard dining chairs, go for those that can do double duty as occasional seating, but keep in

mind that designs with arms should be able to tuck away under the table. Add tie-on cushions or look for padded cane or Lloyd loom chairs that are easy to move around.

Although not as inviting as chairs, benches – freestanding or built-in – take up less space and, again, allow extra bodies to be squeezed in. Children seem to like this informal seating style, and are usually agile enough to scramble in and out of the middle. If you decide on built-in benches, add storage underneath.

Try to provide a separate lighting source for your dining table, both so you can see well enough to serve and eat your meal, and to draw attention away from the rest of the room. A rise-and-fall fitting with a dimmer switch gives the greatest flexibility, but if you choose a fixed pendant, site it low enough so the beam is concentrated on the table, yet high enough so conversation doesn't have to be carried on around the shade.

LEFT *Choose right-angled or parallel benches to fit in the maximum number of diners. If your table is long and narrow, look for an old church pew in an antique or junk shop.*

RIGHT *Low shelves, painted to match the walls and ceiling and filled with china, conceal the cooking area in this small kitchen/dining room. The round, marble-topped table has a pedestal base to keep the floor clear.*

BATHROOMS

Over the previous generation, our feelings about the bathroom seem to have become much more positive, so that we now see it as a room where we can relax and pamper ourselves, rather than as a bleak cold place where we regularly perform spartan rituals. There is no reason why a tiny bathroom cannot be as pleasant and inviting as a large one, and there are lots of ways you can bring this about.

If your flat has been carved out of part of an older house, you may find there is a separate bathroom and toilet, and you would gain considerable space by knocking these into one. If you live alone, this is probably the best solution, but if there are several people in the household, it might be preferable to leave things as they are so that each function can be used without tying up the other one.

Once you've established the space you have to work with, you'll have to sort out where the major fittings are to go and which fittings you want. Naturally the toilet and the basin are indispensable, but you may want to replace the bath with a

ABOVE RIGHT *A huge slab of wall-fixed mirror opens out this tiny pink-washed room and makes a row of pot plants look like a mini-conservatory. Ugly pipes have been boxed in to make a low shelf for storage.*

shower to make room for a bidet or a washer/drier, or simply to squeeze in a bathroom where there wouldn't otherwise be room. In a really restricted area, consider lining the room with tiles, fixing the shower into the wall and putting the drainage hole in the floor itself, so you can do away with tray, cabinet and curtains altogether.

The cheapest and easiest way to position fittings (and keep runs of pipework to a minimum) is to put them as near as possible to their relevant water supply or soil outlet, but if another arrangement makes better use of space, it's perfectly possible to adapt the plumbing to make it feasible. To help you make these decisions, many sanitaryware manufacturers produce catalogues that contain not only a printed grid, on which you can draw your room (indicating where water comes in and soil goes out), but also scaled-down push-out shapes representing each fitting available. When you are moving these shapes around, keep in mind the suggested minimum areas that should surround each one for comfortable use: alongside

LEFT *Make the best use of space in an attic conversion by siting the bath and basin under a sloping ceiling. If you can't fix a mirror for grooming in the usual place, look for one on an extending arm that can be pulled into position when it's needed.*

the bath, you need 110 × 70cm (3ft 8in × 2ft 4in); in front of the basin, 110cm (3ft 8in) in width and 65cm (2ft 2in) in depth so you can bend over it comfortably; WCs and bidets need an area 75cm (3ft) wide and 55cm (1ft 10in) deep. If you have a separate shower, try to leave a space 90 × 70cm (3ft × 2ft 4in) in front of it. Since in a very small bathroom it is unlikely that more than one fitting will be used at a time, these areas can overlap.

If you can spare the floor space, bring the bath out from the wall to the width of one row of tiles to provide a very useful shelf for toiletries.

RIGHT *If your bath or shower cubicle is reasonably wide, contain splashes with a clear panel, which is almost invisible. In a restricted shower area however, you may find a conventional curtain less confining.*

Fittings

To keep the bathroom warm, dry and fresh, adequate heating and ventilation are essential. First, swap any existing radiator for a heated towel rail; this should be more than adequate for a little room, but if it needs topping up, look for a ceiling-mounted light and heater combined, operated from a pull cord.

To prevent condensation and remove unpleasant odours, install an extractor fan. Most building regulations insist you have such a system in internal bathrooms, but they are a good idea even when

floor-standing models. Even the most minute room will look larger if the floor is completely clear, and it will be much easier to clean as well – an important consideration here. Choosing your basin in this style is a particularly good idea since you can fix it at the most appropriate height for you, and make use of the area underneath for storage. You'll need a strong wall to support your fittings however, and some plumbing (especially that for the WC) may be slightly more complicated, but you should find any trouble or extra expense worthwhile, since so

there is a window, since opening it in cold weather will increase the risk of condensation and let out valuable heat.

As with kitchen units, there are both aesthetic and practical advantages to selecting a wall-mounted WC, basin and bidet rather than

much of the plumbing is concealed, giving a much neater effect.

WCs The simplest, smallest WC is known as a wash-down type, and it uses only the force of the water from the cistern. A slightly bulkier design, known as syphonic, has a

ABOVE LEFT *To avoid feeling claustrophobic in a Lilliputian lavatory or bathroom, use the same material for the floor and the walls, extending it right up to the ceiling. Here, even the unusually deep window sill and reveals have been given the tiled treatment.*

ABOVE *Turn an existing cloakroom into a second bathroom by installing a recessed basin and a short bath, panelled with tongue and groove cladding to suggest width. A pale, all-over colour scheme like this one can always be counted on to give a more spacious feel.*

more sophisticated operation that actually sucks the contents of the bowl away as well. Within these two types, there is no appreciable difference in bowl size between one make and another, but if space is really crucial, it's worth checking around. There *are* variations though, in the size and position of the cistern, so look for a special slim version, or choose one that is lower than average if you want to fit it under a window. A flat top rather than the more usual curved one will provide shelf space; remember to put the lid down after use to prevent bottles and jars falling in the pan.

If your plans to install an extra WC are frustrated because it's not possible to install a large soil pipe, invest in an electrical macerator that fixes to a horizontal outlet and compacts soil so it will go through a much narrower one.

Baths and showers Most standard sanitaryware ranges include baths of several different sizes, so you have a good chance of finding one to suit your room. Where storage facilities are at a premium, choose a design that is even shorter than the

RIGHT *A boring bathroom has been turned into a nautical fantasy by spray painting the walls silver and studding them with tacks to look like metal sheeting. A frenzel lens in a circular plywood frame looks amazingly like a porthole, especially with a strip of blue film taped across it.*

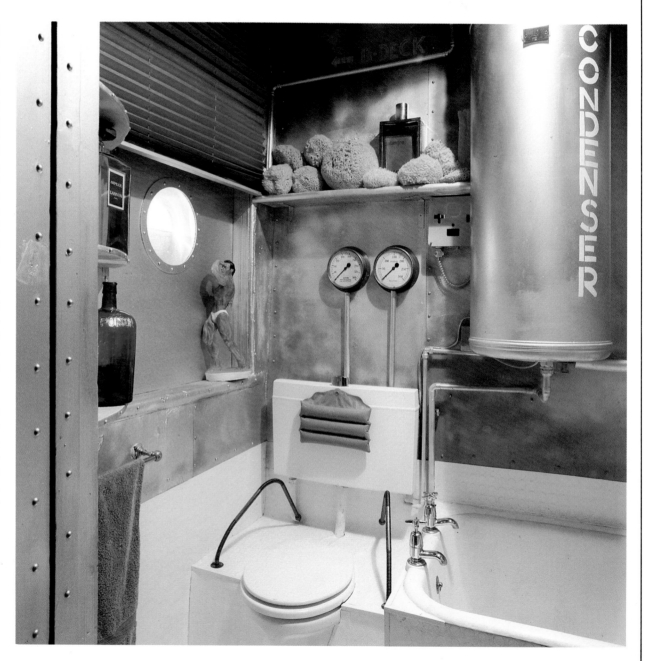

LEFT *For a streamlined look, conceal the WC cistern and waste pipe behind a false panel, making sure to provide some means of access for repairs. This arrangement can also give you a useful shelf for toiletries.*

ABOVE *Fixing taps in the middle, rather than at the end, of the bath allows you to fit in a slightly longer model. It also makes it possible to bathe two children without any arguments about who gets the tap end.*

space available, so you can put a tiled shelf at one end for shampoo and soap. In a long, thin bathroom, your wisest choice might be a modestly sized corner model; these provide an adequate bathing area, yet are shorter overall than a standard shape, which would leave a narrow, useless corridor and visually reinforce the room's awkward shape.

The most space-saving baths of all are no more than 100cm (3ft 4in) square, yet deep enough so you can sit in them and be totally immersed. Some of these are flat on the bottom, while others have built-in seats; you can even install a shower attachment high on the wall to provide a choice of washing facilities.

Those who are attracted by a whirlpool bath or jacuzzi will be reassured to learn that these can be installed in even the smallest fitting.

You can often gain considerable space by putting in a shower instead of a bath (you'll save time and water too), but before you opt for this solution, either make sure there is enough natural pressure from the hot-water tank for its operation, or invest in one with a mechanism that heats water as it passes through. In a tight corner, choose shower curtains rather than rigid panels that might get in the way of your elbows as you reach up to lather your hair.

Basins More than any other bathroom fitting, basins are available in

a very wide range of shapes and sizes, including positively microscopic ones designed to tuck in the corner of a cloakroom or be recessed into its wall. Before you leap upon one of these as the answer to your problems however, remember that not only are they often too small to take standard taps, they are also completely useless for anything but rinsing hands. Unless you are equipping an additional bathroom whose basin will never be needed for washing hair or clothes, try to save space in another way, perhaps by choosing a wide oval shape that takes up very little room from front to back, or a squarish model if width is restricted.

A basin that is boxed in underneath will take up extra actual and visual space, but it may offer enough storage capacity to make this worthwhile.

Taps Most baths and basins are available without tap holes to give you the option of plumbing into the wall, thus freeing the area around the fitting and making it easier to clean. Wall-mounting your taps over the bath is a particularly good idea since it allows you to save space by positioning them in the middle or in a corner rather than at the end. If you want mixer taps, those made for the bathroom, like kitchen models, come in a compact, single-lever, monobloc version as well as the more familiar design with two separate, but joined, units.

Storage

Even the largest, or the most cleverly laid-out, bathroom will look cluttered and messy if it's strewn with hairpins and combs, jars and bottles, toilet rolls and tins of cleanser, so it's particularly important to come to grips with these necessities in a poky one.

If wall space is in short supply, look for a medicine cabinet with a mirror on the front, rather than having two separate items. Fix a row of shelves next to it and keep everyday items handy but contained in serried ranks of different sized wicker baskets, plastic storage bins or even a cutlery tray. Whenever possible, choose wall-mounted storage accessories – obvious things like a toothbrush rack and soap dish and more unusual ones like a tissue box holder. Steal a tip from the kitchen and fix a hanging grid system of some kind for backbrushes, bath caps and bags holding soap supplies and seldom-used toilet articles. Fix a shelf (or even a cupboard) high on the wall to hold extra toilet rolls, towels and dangerous medicines (in a pretty

box or basket maybe), and trailing plants that will appreciate the room's steamy atmosphere and add a decorative touch. Shelves are very useful over the bath as well – perhaps triangular ones in a corner – but make sure everything you need while you're in it is stored within easy reach to avoid accidents.

Keep face flannels (washcloths)

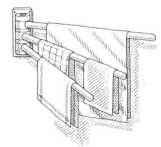

handy on a swing-out tea-towel rack or a row of small rubber discs. When it comes to towels, rings are really the most space-saving arrangement but bath towels can't dry properly in them and are tricky to get in and out. Try fixing a single wooden pole or a length of chrome tubing along one whole wall near (or above) the bath, or a row of either between two uprights at the

ABOVE *Look for a basin with integral storage, or fix shelves or drawers under a wall-mounted design. Bathroom, as well as kitchen, taps are available in compact, monobloc versions.*

LEFT *Make use of space that is usually wasted by storing the proliferation of towels, cleaning supplies, toilet rolls, tissues and medicines in a run of capacious, high-level cupboards. If there are children in evidence, fit doors with locks to keep dangerous drugs and chemicals out of harm's way.*

end, giving it a built-in look and providing drying space for hand washing as well as towels. A small, simple ladder, painted to match the walls, would do the job – you can make one from lengths of dowelling.

If there is any floor space available, buy two small wastepaper bins – one for used tissues and packaging, the other to hold scouring powder, bleach etc. A laundry bin – especially one that doubles as a stool – is ideal for dirty clothes and linen, but if such a thing can't be accommodated, buy (or sew) a large bag to hang on the back of the door. Most bathroom doors are fitted with a hook, but see if yours has room for two, either side by side or one above the other.

RIGHT *Install your basin in a wide vanity unit that has been tiled all over to match the floor, the walls, and the bath surround. Keep pretty towels in open baskets, motley grooming aids in closed ones.*

Decoration

Like all other rooms, your smallest one will benefit from an all-over treatment, at least in colour if not in material. Go for plain tiles, and instead of stopping them halfway, take them right up the wall and paint the ceiling to match, or treat any wall above them in the same way; use a high-gloss finish to echo their shine. You'll achieve a very streamlined look if you build in chunky shelves first, then tile right over them, and go on to cover the bath and basin surrounds. Box in any ugly pipe runs and cover the resulting shelf with your chosen tiles or painted finish.

Avoid adding a lot of fussy details, like frilled or bordered curtains and blinds, but don't be afraid to risk a single sensational one like a quirky collection of postcards or objects, or even a huge cartoon seaside mural that will open up the space dramatically. Although an outrageous scheme will soon pall in general living areas, it could add a welcome touch of irreverence in a room like this, which is occupied for short periods only.

Finally, don't ruin the effect you've created by draping the room with a motley collection of towels in different colours and patterns. If you're equipping a new home, select one plain colour and stick to it; if your bathroom linen is already a ragbag, it's a fairly simple task to dye the whole collection to match.

LEFT *This dazzling all-white scheme has been relieved with witty touches of black: a strip of skirting, a bold stripe on the towels, and a tiled frieze, carried on across the blind and reflected in the huge mirror.*

RIGHT *Timber cladding has many advantages in a bathroom: it offers excellent heat and noise insulation, and conceals unsightly plumbing. Before you choose it however, be sure your walls are free from damp, and seal the wood with polyurethane to keep out moisture and prevent rot.*

FAR RIGHT *Transport a mundane bathroom to the seaside by painting (or commissioning) a space-expanding trompe l'oeil mural.*

BEDROOMS

Many of us see our bedrooms primarily as providing us with a private, peaceful sanctuary at the end of the day. In a very small home however, we are sometimes forced to balance this psychological need against the huge demands made on other areas; certainly, leaving the whole room empty and unused for almost all of every day seems illogical. It may be that by rearranging the furniture and adding a desk, or building-in a work area, you could enlist it to do double duty as a study, a craft or hobby room, or even a second sitting room, perhaps with a stereo or a portable television. At very least, try to provide a comfortable chair, a good reading light and maybe an extra kettle so you'll have a corner of your own where you can retire from the hurly-burly of family activities.

Your bedroom will have an atmosphere more appropriate to general living if you get rid of any aggressively boudoirish decorations and organize concealed storage for your toiletries.

You'll be grateful for a small hand basin here, as will other members of the household who are regularly held up by your morning ablutions. Choose a minute cloakroom model if that's all you have room for, and hide it behind a simple screen. To keep a full-length mirror unobtrusive, fix it to the back of the door, inside a closet or wardrobe, or on a wall behind the screen that conceals your basin.

Decide first where you want the bed, since this is probably the largest, most awkward item. Although many people dislike the hemmed-in feeling of sleeping against a wall, you'll almost certainly get the most from your space if the bed is in this position – perhaps even tucked in a corner. Make sure such a bed rolls out on castors, and has a fitted undersheet and a duvet so bedmaking is quick and easy.

You should be able to use each item of furniture comfortably without risk of bumping into anything else. Leave a 75cm (2ft 6in) corridor next to, or around, your bed, or 95cm (3ft 2in) if closet or wardrobe doors open into the same space. Twin beds should have a minimum of 50cm (1ft 8in) between them. A dressing table needs 60cm (2ft) in front if it has a knee recess, 90cm (3ft) if there isn't one. Allow 95cm (3ft 2in) clearance in front of a chest of drawers, a closet or a wardrobe.

LEFT *Free space in a tiny bedroom by sleeping against the wall. Here, the cosy, closed-in feeling is reinforced by curtaining the bed with richly-coloured kelims; a low mirror at the head fights incipient claustrophobia.*

RIGHT *In a similarly-sized room, the same tactic has been used, yet the effect is open and airy, largely because of the crisp white scheme. To extend the room visually, choose a high bed, and make sure its cover clears the floor completely.*

Storage

In this room, the eternal fitted-vs-freestanding storage quandary is at its most acute. Unlike the living room, where 'fitted storage' can simply mean a run of open shelves, bedroom requirements are much more complex, since accommodation is needed for hanging and folded garments of all shapes and sizes; for odd-shaped accessories, for small things like jewellery, and often for an unwieldy mass of grooming paraphernalia as well.

Like built-in fittings anywhere else, those you buy for the bedroom are fairly expensive, they cannot change their position or be taken with you when you move, and they will influence your decorating style for a long time to come. On the plus side, they make excellent use of space and give an elegant, streamlined appearance. At their most expensive (and often their most efficient), these are custom-designed and made by a specialist firm. Less expensive are ready-made fittings that come in many different sizes and styles, but they

are unlikely to fit your room precisely, even by using the filler units that are part of most ranges, and their internal fittings have not been chosen with your needs in mind. The cheapest built-in alternative is to do the planning and construction yourself. Use the walls of an under-sized room as the unit's back and sides; instead of standard doors that take up a great deal of space, fit folding or sliding ones (though the latter prevent you from viewing your whole wardrobe at once). Better still, do away with doors altogether, and fix blinds or just a simple curtain.

Freestanding items, usually a wardrobe and a chest of drawers, or perhaps a dressing table, offer much greater flexibility in the room's arrangement and are more likely to suit a traditional scheme.

Whichever storage system you end up with, it will work better for you if you give as much thought to the inside of it as you have to the room as a whole. Approach the problem by deciding first what you can do without – any item you

LEFT If there is no clearance space for ordinary wardrobe or cupboard doors, replace them with those on a sliding mechanism. Alternatively, divide a single, hinged door on a fitted cupboard into two sections, stable fashion, so the largest part is at the top. You can then use all the available floor space by positioning the bed (or a low table) right against the cupboard, yet

still gain access to the hanging rail; store boxes full of seldom-worn garments underneath.

RIGHT This rustic retreat contains no furniture at all apart from the bed; fitted shelves and cupboards provide storage for small items around the headboard, built-in wardrobes span the room at the other end.

haven't worn during the last year is an obvious contender. Now look at exactly what needs to be accommodated. Mostly dresses and coats that require full-length hanging space? Formal gowns that are even longer? Suits, shirts, blouses and skirts? Folded sweaters that need to be stored so one can be extracted without disturbing the rest of the pile? A shoe collection of Imeldian proportions? Take some of the pressure off by storing out-of-season clothes, accessories and footwear elsewhere.

Group all the remaining hanging articles together by length. Most hangers need a depth of 50cm (1ft 8in); street-length garments require clearance of about 150cm (5ft), while floor-length ones should have 180cm (6ft). Separates however are little more than half this length, 100cm (3ft 4in), so use the space under them for a shoe rack, storage boxes, laundry bin or low shelf for boots and bags. Or borrow a stacking vegetable rack from the kitchen for such awkward items. If your unit is high enough, you could even fix another hanging rail underneath the first, doubling its capacity.

LEFT *Design your own sleeping/ storage wall to exploit space at every level. The small tables that slot under the mattress in this ingenious unit offer desk facilities as well as a place to enjoy crumb-free breakfasts in bed.*

Look for special hangers that hold several skirts or pairs of trousers rather than just one, or those that keep ties untangled and accessible. Alternatively, screw a row of hooks inside your wardrobe or closet that will organize not only ties, but scarves, belts, necklaces and small bags. On the back of the door fix a plastic or fabric shoe bag

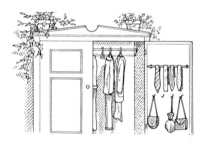

with rows of pockets to keep each pair separate, and safe from scuffs and scratches.

If there are none there already, try to find room for a few shelves, along the top or down one side, to take hats, bulky sweaters, or small baskets, trays or transparent food storage boxes for toiletries and jewellery. Make sure any shelves in

ABOVE *Bedside clutter is contained on a butler's tray and a pedestal table, both of which combine a generous surface area with an unobtrusive base. Lights are wall fixed to give better-placed illumination, spotlight two American primitive portraits, and keep the table-tops clear.*

LEFT *Gain an impression of space by concealing a pair of uplighters behind your bed – perhaps positioned across a corner instead of against a wall.*

a purpose-built unit are adjustable, and supplement them with clip-on or pull-out wire baskets.

If it suits your scheme, choose some of your most dramatic pieces – an exotic kimono or shawl, an assortment of zany hats, or an unusually pretty bracelet collection – and hang them on the wall, making a kind of working display area.

If your main storage system does not contain drawers or baskets of some kind, you'll have to provide a home for small items elsewhere. A chest of drawers is the most usual choice; make sure yours has small, shallow drawers as well as large deep ones, since it's very hard to store bras, pants, and socks neatly in a cavernous space suitable for thick woollens. Alternatively, look at items of furniture designed for another purpose altogether; a small dresser (or hutch) could hold books, hats and toiletries on the open shelving at the top, underwear in one or two drawers, and shoes in a cupboard below.

Since you'll need a table surface of some description by your bed, choose one that provides extra storage underneath. As well as purpose-made bedside tables, have a look at small chests of drawers; cane, wooden, or metal trunks; or, in modern schemes, low metal filing cabinets, which are now sold in an exciting and non-officey range of colours. Keep in mind though, that this surface should not be much higher or lower than the mattress for most convenient use. You could even do without a table here, and fix a simple shelf to the wall beside your bed, leaving the floor area clear, or choose an extended bedhead with shelves cantilevered out from it on either side.

Temporary tactics For many students, or young people in rented accommodation, any major item of storage furniture is out of reach financially and inappropriate in any case, since they may have no interest in accumulating bulky possessions. In this situation, the cheapest and most efficient – as well as the most portable – way of dealing with an overflow of clothes is by investing in a metal rail designed for use in shops and offices, and available at outlets specializing in retail display equipment. Fitted with castors and easy to dismantle for relocation, one of these will take care of all your hanging needs and can be hidden from view behind a decorative screen or curtain.

LEFT *Do away with tables altogether by replacing the bedhead with narrow shelves to take lamps, pictures and night-time paraphernalia.*

RIGHT *Turn a teenager's bedroom into a private living room by installing a stylish sofa bed, plenty of storage facilities, and audio equipment for entertainment. Make use of high-level space to store old books or even out-of-season clothing in pretty boxes or wicker hampers.*

ABOVE *Search out an old mantel mirror to make a striking headboard in a traditional room. This one has been painted white to match the bed's coverlet and the pile of frosty lace cushions on top. To show off an unusual pattern of glazing bars on the casement window, and to let in the* maximum amount of light, curtains have been left off altogether – the original shutters fold out at night. Below the picture rail, a delicately patterned pink wallpaper focuses interest on the lower part of the room, which could have looked disproportionately tall.

Beds

Ordinary freestanding beds are 190cm (6ft 3in) or 200cm (6ft 6in) long, and come in three basic widths: single (approximately 90cm [3ft]), small double (135cm [4ft 6in]), and large double (150cm [5ft]); if yours must sleep two people, think twice about settling for a small double to save space, since it will allow each occupant only the width of a baby's cot. If you're willing to pay over the odds however, have one specially made that is an in-between width, or shorter than standard; if this means you can fit it across a tiny box room, or in an alcove, the extra cost might be worthwhile. In terms of height, you may have to trade off practicality for appearance. A very low design will make an oppressively low room feel loftier, but it will also deprive you of one of the most traditional hidden storage areas – under the bed. You'll lose out on both counts if you go for a high divan with an ordinary deep base, so choose either a mattress on slats or springs that leaves enough room underneath for your own *ad hoc* storage arrangements (suitcases etc.) or a deep divan base that contains built-in storage facilities; some have drawers or sliding doors along the side, at the base, or both, and these need to be surrounded by enough space so they can be operated easily. Others feature a mattress that lifts up from the end or from one side to give access to a roomy area underneath. This type needs less room around it, but its contents are also less accessible.

To exploit the area under the bed even more fully, buy only the mattress and build in your own base at whatever height and width you require. Fix a large 'shelf' across one end of the room at waist level for example, and make it slightly wider than your mattress to give you an adjacent surface for bedside necessities. (It's very important that any solid mattress base is drilled for ventilation to prevent damp and mildew.) Now fit out the space underneath with shelves for small articles, or leave it open for camping or sports equipment and luggage. Add simple steps for access and conceal your glory hole behind doors, blinds or curtains.

If you have no talent for carpentry, place your mattress on a low base of storage cubes but again, make sure they can be drilled for ventilation.

You'll get the maximum possible use from this area if you put your bed on a high platform, leaving the 'room' underneath open for a desk or seating, or concealing it to make a walk-in wardrobe. Build this from wood or, if the high-tech look appeals to you, look for a purpose-made version in tubular steel and wire mesh. These are often supplied in kit form to be assembled on site, thus avoiding transportation or access problems. A cheaper, but more complicated, alternative would be to design and make one of these yourself using metal scaffolding and clamps.

Whatever your platform is made from, you must make absolutely certain that your floor can take the weight of such a structure.

LEFT *Don't let the size of a room – or its location – prevent you from exploring the style of your choice. This modestly proportioned study/bedroom overlooks the traffic on Broadway, yet achieves all the elegance of the Biedermeier period that inspired it. During the day, the cherry wood sleigh-bed is upholstered in corduroy so it can be used for seating; at night, the owner sleeps between two duvets covered in white linen, which are easy to toss into place, then remove the next morning.*

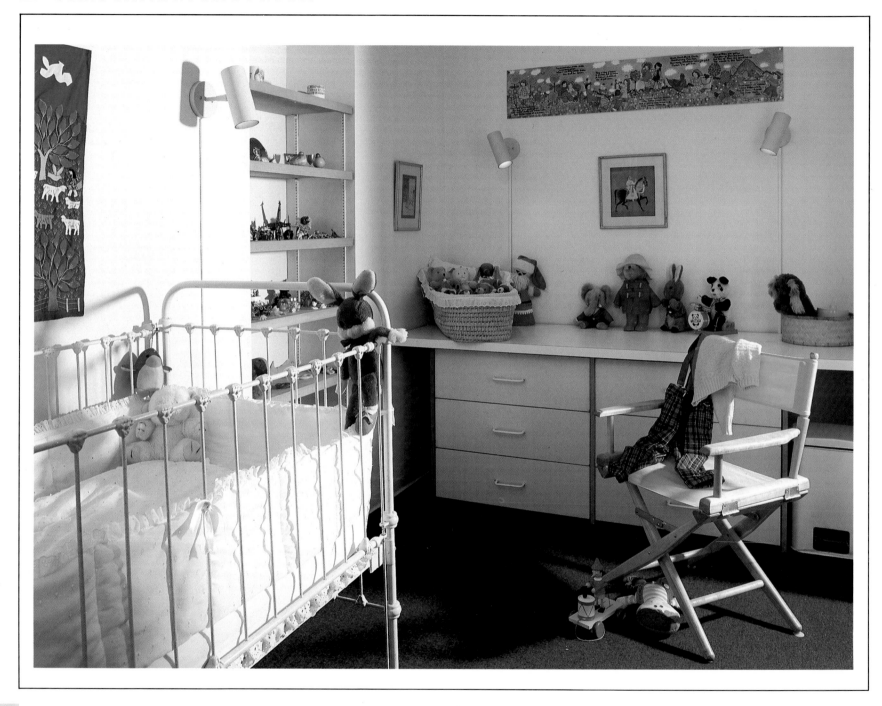

CHILDREN'S ROOMS

Any investment of time, thought and cash you make in your offspring's habitat will pay double dividends: to the room's occupant, who will be happy to play, work and entertain as well as sleep there, and to you, who will be able to relax in a quiet, tidy living room without being crowded out by youthful mayhem.

Whatever the age of your child, avoid decorating the room in an aggressively juvenile way. First, because such a scheme will be outgrown before it needs replacing, and secondly, so the room can be pressed into service as occasional guest accommodation. If you start off with a neutral scheme, the room will look bigger and neater, and quickly evolving tastes can be catered for without undue upheaval or expense. To make changes in surroundings even easier, cover one whole wall with a pinboard to form a constantly varying display area. Apply blackboard paint to the back of the door, minimizing danger to the walls, and saving the space that would be taken up by even a floor-standing model.

Resist special, scaled-down furniture – although it would seem to be ideal for small spaces, it is, in reality, useful for only a short time before it becomes redundant or worse, resented. Look instead for items that will adapt and grow with their owner: a single wardrobe into which you can fix shelves above or below the hanging level of scaled-

LEFT *A room that is decorated using neutral colours, and equipped with sturdy, full-sized furniture, will accommodate the tastes, activities and storage requirements of a child from babyhood to teenage years.*

ABOVE *Built-in bunk beds provide sleeping facilities for two in an undersized bedroom. Mesh panels act as safety rails and give the design a high-tech look; access is provided by a miniature staircase that doubles as bedside tables.*

down garments, or a sturdy low coffee table that is just the right height for a kneeling toddler.

Almost more than in an adult's room, a washbasin here will be invaluable – for sluicing down a baby during changing; for cleaning up after messy activities like painting; and for use in endless teenage grooming sessions and coffee making, thus easing congestion in both bathroom and kitchen.

If table space is lacking, fit a bedside light into the wall, an arrangement that will also prevent it from being knocked over by a tired child.

Beds

The most popular sleeping provision when there are two children in one room is bunk beds – youngsters like their enclosed, cabin-like feeling as much as parents appreciate their space-saving qualities. This set-up has much to recommend it for a single sleeper as well, since it allows a friend to stay overnight, while the bottom bunk, kitted out with lots of throw cushions, will serve as seating during the day. Look for those that can detach to become separate freestanding beds later on – some even have storage drawers as well. The most important factor in choosing any bunk bed is safety – make sure the access ladder is stable, the safety rail is secure, and the distance between this rail and the mattress is not so narrow that a sleepy little head could become trapped.

PLATFORM BED page 132

On the other hand, small persons subject to vertigo would be better off with a trundle bed, which rolls out on castors from under a standard model (being slightly smaller), and often includes a mechanism that raises it up to the same height.

In a room so minute that even a single bed seems to fill it, consider one that folds up and away into a cupboard (or behind a curtain) during the day, leaving the floor area free for play. This design is sometimes known as a Murphy bed, and the best-designed of these can stay made up, so you don't have to strip the sheets and blankets every morning.

Even in the most undersized rooms, small guests could sleep on two floor cushions pushed together, or in a sleeping bag that rolls up to make a squidgy bolster when it's not in use.

Storage

Like adults, children will be much more inclined to keep their surroundings tidy if there is ample and convenient storage provision for their possessions. The key here is accessibility – especially for small children, the most obvious way to clear a room of toys and games is to toss them all into a capacious receptacle like a wooden crate, a wicker log basket, or even a full-sized rub-bish bin (garbage can), preferably in brightly coloured plastic or shiny metal that looks exciting and can handle a great deal of rough treatment without showing any damage. A large, flat-topped blanket box would fulfil the same function, and do double duty as extra seating if you add a fitted cushion.

For small toys and books, provide a set of inexpensive stacking vegetable racks, again in bright

colours. Make or buy a tough canvas wall pocket, which, again, will adapt to a child's changing needs.

Install a floor-to-ceiling wall storage system for books and records, perhaps with a wide shelf at desk height to provide a work surface without taking up unnecessary floor space. If two children share, place the beds against facing walls, and provide storage and privacy with a dividing unit.

FAR LEFT *Provide low-level toy storage in the form of simple wooden boxes that roll away on castors. In future years, these will be useful for shoes, bags and sports equipment.*

LEFT *An industrial shelving system caters stylishly for the needs of a busy teenager. When he moves out, it can be dismantled and taken with him.*

RIGHT *Extensive and treasured collections will stay neat and undamaged in small shelves or sets of drawers like these.*

HALLS AND STAIRS

While you are busy dreaming up ways to make your rooms look more attractive and work harder, don't neglect the considerable potential of the connecting areas between them.

Halls and landings

The most precious halls and landings are those than can be adapted for occasional use as an extra room. If possible, install a table that takes up very little space during household rush hours, but can be expanded to provide a larger surface when traffic is light – perhaps a console design with a fold-out top, a gate-leg model, or a flap-down or flap-up surface attached to the wall.

Even in the tiniest hall, try to provide some kind of surface, maybe only a single shelf, to take

post, keys, gloves and messages. At a pinch, a pretty basket or perhaps a wire or wicker bicycle pannier hung near (or on) the door will do this job. A good-sized mirror will make the dingiest hall look bigger and brighter, and allow for last-minute grooming, while a row of hooks

ABOVE *Make an extensive larder from a wasted corridor by lining it with narrow shelves that hold one or two rows of crockery and provisions (making everything easy to locate), yet will not impede traffic.*

RIGHT *Turn a spare bedroom into an almost-self-contained flat for a teenager or elderly relation by installing a miniature kitchen on a nearby landing or hall.*

keeps coats, jackets and hats in the most convenient location and removes the bulkiest items from closets and wardrobes elsewhere. Discipline yourself to pack away out-of-season outdoor clothing so these garments don't take over.

Almost every hall and landing has some storage potential beyond obvious things like these however. Make yours into a mini-library by lining it with narrow shelves; most purpose-made bookcases are 30cm (12in) deep, and many are deeper still, yet few non-illustrated books need more than 15cm (6in), and paperbacks even less. Store larger volumes on deeper shelves fixed above head level so they don't restrict the area's width. Even if you don't require quite so much storage of this kind, deep high shelves along any hall would be useful for large items you don't use often. If the ceiling is lofty enough, you could even span it with slats of wood or strong bamboo poles, which would support boxes and baskets full of junk, and even act as hanging rails at the same time. An unusually high ceiling would also allow you to rig up a pulley system so awkwardly shaped articles like a bicycle or skis could be hoisted out of the way when they're not required.

Stairs

If you are able to make structural changes to your home, altering the design or the position of your stairs could make a dramatic impact on its

efficiency and its appearance. It may be, for example, that you can free a large enough space for a shower or laundry room by replacing a straight flight with quarter-turn, dog-leg or spiral ones, all of which take up not necessarily less, but differently shaped, squarer space. In general, the greater the distance between floors, the more space you can save. Again, check out local building regulations covering headroom, pitch, width of treads, and height of risers, and make sure you provide enough illumination for the stairs to be used safely.

The smallest spiral staircase that most building regulations would approve for access to living areas is about 140cm (4ft 8in) wide overall, and this could be ideal for an attic bedroom or study. You'll need a slightly wider spiral to replace the home's main staircase, but if all you need is access to a storage area, you can install a suitable design as narrow as 90cm (3ft).

Where no structural change is possible or worthwhile, you can often lighten the appearance of your stairway, and make the hall look less claustrophobic, by choosing one that has open rather than solid risers, and exposing the area under-neath. Once again, you will have to balance aesthetic advantages against functional ones, since a built-in cup-board here would be very valuable for storing awkwardly shaped clean-ing equipment or carpentry tools. Perhaps you could compromise by

leaving it mostly clear, with only a row of shallow bookshelves fixed to the wall, or by using this space for a single mattress on an unobtrusively low platform, which would provide accommodation for overnight guests. Disguise it with a simple cover and throw cushions in the

same colour as the floor covering.

At the top of the house, construct a strong, deep shelf or cupboard across the stairwell. Although this may not be accessible without a ladder, it might be the only place available in a pocket-sized home to store large suitcases, camping equipment, family memorabilia, Christmas decorations and other things you are unlikely to use more than once a year.

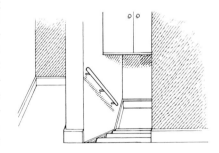

ABOVE *An under-used hall (perhaps leading to a side door) might be adapted to house a miniature laundry area if you stack the tumble drier on top of the washing machine. If this is too ambitious, try at least to gain a small home-office area or even an extra cupboard here.*

RIGHT *When stairs open directly on to a top floor room, use the dead space above them by spanning it with a deep, wide work surface. For an uncluttered*

look, make sure this is the same colour as the adjoining wall.

FAR RIGHT *Even if your stairway or hall can't fill any practical function, give yourself a stimulating change of view by turning it into a gallery of changing visual images – hang inexpensive things like posters, photographs, attractive packaging, printed bags and record sleeves as well as more conventional ones such as framed pictures and mirrors.*

MULTI-PURPOSE ROOMS

Even when you have a big enough home for a separate room to be allotted to each main activity – living, sleeping, cooking and washing – there are likely to be several additional functions clamouring for a space of their own.

If you have a spare room to absorb some of this overflow, organize it so it serves at least two purposes. To do this, first look at the demands each will make on the space available; you won't be pursuing a hobby or doing paperwork while you have a house guest for example, so combine a study and guest room by fitting out a spare bedroom with a single bed, plus a desk or built-in work surface with shelves above and a chair that tucks underneath. A visitor is not going to need much hanging space, so a coat-rack or a row of hooks would do, and one table light could serve as both desk and bedside illumination. In a box room, rig up a large work surface that flaps down to cover the bed.

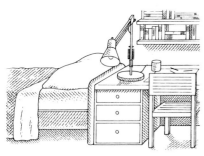

A slightly larger room could act as a dining area as well, with a table pulled into the centre of the room for meals, then pushed against the wall to become a desk or dressing table. Chairs could stack in a corner or hang up. Multi-purpose furniture comes into its own in this situation, so if a full-sized bed is out of the question, go for a small sofa bed, or a convertible chair or pouffe (ottoman).

An old-fashioned scullery or utility room is a natural place for a laundry, and maybe you can tie this up with another activity that involves water, like wine-making. Or set up a sewing corner here, where the ironing board is always handy; one generous work surface will take your equipment and provide a place to sort and fold clothes.

Quick studies

Even when there are no spare rooms, try to commandeer a built-in cupboard or closet as a study or hobby area by installing a wall-to-wall work surface inside with shelves above it and a pinboard in between. If you need a larger desk, fix a work surface that is hinged vertically so you can pull it down when the door is open.

At very least, try to find some permanent home office nook in the living room, bedroom or kitchen, perhaps just a corner shelf.

LEFT *This home-based office turns into a comfortable guest room when the sofa-bed is fully extended. To clear enough floor area, part of the work surface flaps down, and the chairs fold neatly away. Note the spotlights fixed to the underside of the open shelves.*

BELOW *The same two functions are combined in a long, narrow room. Here, a low platform separates the work space from the adjoining sleeping/sitting area.*

To establish what could be done with the attic and the basement, first check local building regulations to see what restrictions they put on 'habitable areas' (living rooms, bedrooms, etc.) in terms of ceiling height, ventilation and so forth. Even if the space you have in mind doesn't qualify, you might be able to install a bathroom, shower or laundry there. At very least, you could greatly increase storage capacity by fitting shelves, bins, racks, hooks or hanging rails to replace tatty cardboard boxes.

When no electricity, heating or plumbing are laid on, the next step will be to explore the feasibility of running these services from the main part of house.

ABOVE LEFT *Make a feature of an attic's dramatic shape by picking out structural supports and window frames in a sharply contrasting colour. The pale monochrome scheme in this top-floor kitchen focuses all the attention upwards.*

ABOVE *Help a converted basement to look as light and spacious as possible by choosing open-tread stairs for access. If the ceiling is in good condition, give it a high-gloss finish that reflects the room and makes it seem higher.*

Attics

If there isn't an existing stairway, remember that you'll lose some space on the floor below when you install one. Where headroom is a problem (and privacy on the top level is not) choose stairs that open directly into the room above. Any insulation between the floorboards

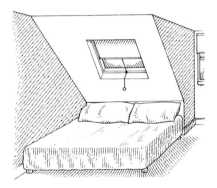

will have to be re-laid between the rafters. In addition, timbers that were not designed to carry weight may need to be reinforced with extra, thicker joists. To increase light, add dormer windows or skylights.

You can make the room's shape look less awkward and increase storage capacity at the same time by fitting cupboards or a work surface under the sloping roof. Any furniture that doesn't require full height for use, such as a sofa, chair or bed, would also suit this restricted space under the eaves.

You can either minimize the room's irregularity by decorating walls, floors and windows in the same neutral way, arranging furniture in neat groups and focusing interest in the centre of the room to draw attention there; or accentuate quirky angles by fixing pictures to sloping walls and covering the floor with brightly patterned rugs placed at unexpected angles.

Basements

The basement is often an excellent site for a study or bedroom since it's naturally insulated from any noise upstairs. The greatest potential stumbling block during conversion is damp, so establish whether any is coming from outside or is the result of condensation, and deal with it appropriately. Then, box in any pipes and panel over rough walls to provide a surface suitable for decorating.

Since any basement is likely to be dark, choose a warm pastel colour rather than pure white, which will look grey and gloomy. If the ceiling is low, keep the furniture low as well to improve the room's proportions visually.

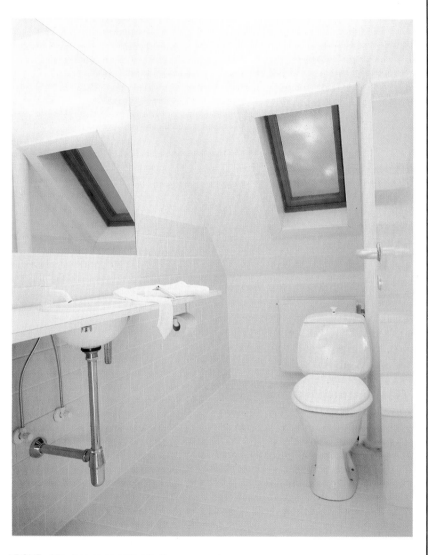

ABOVE *Alleviate congestion in the family bathroom by squeezing an extra one into the attic or basement. This can be much simpler than siting a bedroom or living room there, since less strict planning regulations frequently apply.*

SPECIAL NEEDS

When a small flat, or a bed-sitting room in a house, is being designed for someone who finds ordinary movement difficult, either because of old age or disability, space problems are compounded. It's not possible here to offer more than a few general points, so if you are undertaking such a conversion, especially if the occupant is severely disabled, you should consult a specialist architect or designer.

For people with walking aids, or just for those who are uncertain of their footing, doors should ideally have an opening width of 80cm (2ft 8in), clear of door stops, door thickness and any bulky fittings. Handles should be easy to grip and strongly secured since they will probably be used for support as well as operation. Double doors, sliding doors, or curtains may work better than conventional designs.

Try to arrange wide traffic paths with no sudden turns, and see that all furniture with sharp corners is tucked out of the way. Avoid any changes of floor level, and don't put down loose rugs that could cause a fall. Sofas and chairs should be generously-proportioned (even if they take up extra room) with high seats that are much easier to get in and out of, plus high, straight backs and sturdy arms for support.

In the kitchen, make sure all cupboards are within easy reach, taking into consideration the occupant's range of movement and, if necessary, provide some means of

sitting at the worktop. Remember to provide extra strong illumination to make up for failing eyesight.

Many older people find an ordinary bath too low. Grab rails may help, or think about installing a sitz bath instead, which is shorter than average, but much deeper, with an integral seat at one end so the bather is completely immersed without having to lie down. Alternatively, go for a shower with a built-in seat that folds down from the wall. Both of these solutions save space, which you may need if a support frame has to be provided around the toilet; these are about 50cm (1ft 8in) wide. A wall-mounted pan is best, since it can be fixed at the right height for comfortable use, but if you can't manage this, fit a raised plastic seat on top of the existing one. Choose a wall-hung basin so you can position it high enough for a tall person to use without bending. A wide, shallow bowl will make face and hair washing more convenient.

Again, a high bed is often the easiest to manage, so raise a built-in model on a ventilated platform with drawers underneath. This arrangement would also do away with the need to clean under the bed – an awkward task when bending is painful. Many of the storage ideas that use space effectively also make the contents of a wardrobe or closet easily accessible for the elderly or the disabled: wire baskets on runners, shallow drawers and low hanging rails, for example.

FAR LEFT *Put a two-element ceramic cook-top at the back of the work surface so that hot, heavy pans do not have to be lifted, but can be pulled forward safely. A wooden handrail fixed along the front gives support and provides a nearby place to hang a walking stick.*

LEFT *Reduce unnecessary movement by storing kitchen equipment on open shelves rather than in cupboards, which could also have handles that are hard to grip. Some purpose-made units come with a large trolley that rolls out from under the work surface to make room for a wheelchair.*

ONE-ROOM LIVING

Even though life in a single room has many advantages – heating bills are low, there is less cleaning to be done, and nothing you need is ever very far away – it used to be that this arrangement was strictly a matter of necessity. For many, this is still the case, but increasingly – and interestingly – people are beginning to choose it, either by moving into a loft or warehouse and leaving the space untouched, or by opening up several small rooms into one large, bright one. In the end, whether you select this way of life, or have it thrust upon you, you face the same basic problems: accommodating a considerable range of services and activities in one room so it is both convenient to use, and attractive and comfortable to live in.

Defining space

First, decide whether you want to leave your room completely open, or divide it into separate areas of activity. If you go for breaking it up, there are several ways you can do this. Bring large pieces of furniture away from the wall – a tall bookcase, a dresser (hutch) or a wardrobe – to mark out rooms within your room, or use lower, but still sizeable, pieces like a sideboard or a high-backed sofa to give the impression of different areas without blocking them off entirely. Hang a curtain from ceiling-fixed track to make a movable wall, or use floor-to-ceiling blinds in the same way. Define the kitchen area with a

ABOVE *Separate activity areas in a one-room home with semi-permanent panels that stop short of the ceiling to avoid giving a hemmed-in feeling. This arrangement offers a purpose-designed work station and conceals office clutter from view.*

RIGHT *Here, the job is done by a low, freestanding 'wall' and a dramatic change of floor level – the bed is set into its own raised platform, which also provides a shelf for storing and displaying books.*

peninsular unit at counter height, which will give you extra work and storage space, and hang a blind above it so you can chat freely to guests while you're preparing a meal, then hide away a sink full of dirty dishes afterwards.

One of the most efficient and flexible ways to break up a large room is with screens. As well as concealing cooking facilities, a washbasin or a cluttered desk, they can be moved around easily to provide an entrance hall, a dining alcove, or a dressing room. Disguise your bed with a screen during the day, and at night move it in front of a nearby small window, which could then be left completely free of curtains or blinds.

The most subtle way of all to define space is at floor level, by raising the sleeping or eating area slightly on an easily-constructed platform, or simply with area rugs – in colours that contrast dramatically with the floor covering in a large room, closely allied tones in a more modest one.

What goes where?

When you are allocating functions to each part of the room, try to keep clothes storage as far as possible from food. Even when you have provided excellent ventilation (and it's vital that you do this in a single room), fabrics absorb odour very quickly. Make sure too that the table you eat from is near the cooking facilities to avoid accidents,

LEFT *More defining devices: a run of low-level storage units, a huge shelf suspended from the ceiling, and translucent blinds that roll out of sight when a through vista is required. Small, light tables can be moved from place to place as required.*

ABOVE *Create a sleeping/sitting/storage corner by placing your mattress on a base made from simply constructed boxes, with holes drilled underneath it for ventilation. Choose a washable bedcover that will take heavy wear and still look smart; this jazzy Fifties-inspired fabric is ideal.*

since fitting your furniture into a restricted space is unlikely to leave very wide traffic paths. This table is bound to be the centre of a multitude of activities, so make extra sure it's a comfortable height for you, with a sturdy construction and a tough surface. In a tight spot, a round or oval one minimizes the risk of bumping into sharp corners. Your coffee table is likely to be called on to fill myriad functions as well, so again, invest in a large, solid one with some kind of storage capacity. As in any undersized room, try to keep surfaces clear by making full use of the walls – choose not only wall-mounted storage and lighting, but a schoolroom clock and a telephone that can be fixed next to a comfortable chair.

A cautionary note. Check out all items of dual-purpose furniture for ease of operation; a few are so well-designed that you will use them every day; some are meant for occasional use only since they're rather trickier; while others have mechanisms so tortuous that they end up wasting time and space as well as the money they cost – a coffee table that needs a screwdriver, two people and 25 minutes to be fixed at dining height is unlikely to be used very often.

Sleeping

When you live in one room, your bed should not only be comfortable; it should also look attractive and unbedroomy during the day

and be easy and convenient for you to fall into at night.

One solution might be a high platform structure, as discussed in the Bedrooms section. Such an arrangement takes up hardly any floor space and keeps the sleeping area completely out of sight. On the minus side, you could find climbing up to bed every night (and down for nocturnal visits to the bathroom) a chore. Even though there should always be enough room for you to sit up in a platform bed, the proximity of the ceiling may induce feelings of claustrophobia.

You may prefer a Murphy bed – one that pulls down from inside a cupboard. Available in a double size, with the hinge mechanism at the head, or as a single model, pulling down from one side, these sometimes come as part of a large wall-storage system that includes shelves, cupboards, drawers and hanging space. Choose one that allows you to leave the bedclothes in place, and make sure your room is arranged so the area occupied by the bed during the night is otherwise left fairly clear and you aren't forced to shift furniture before you can retire.

Investigate the enormous range of sofa beds available; to find one that is pretty, comfortable and convenient to use, you'll probably have to look near the top of the market. Avoid any design where the mattress is folded up when not in use since this will quickly cause

MULTI-PURPOSE COFFEE TABLE page 126　PLATFORM BED page 132

LEFT *To liberate as much floor space as possible, remove all storage facilities – hanging rails, shelves, drawers and hooks – to a single wall, then conceal them with blinds, curtains or sliding doors. These are covered with easy-to-fix mirror tiles.*

damage. Some designs have a cover that doubles as a duvet – a good idea if you don't mind sleeping under linen that has been sat on all day. Think twice before you plan to put such a duvet in a separate cover every night however – you may quickly tire of this task.

One type of bed that is frequently sold as a sofa bed (although it can, of course, be used just for sleeping) is a futon – a sort of bedroll that the Japanese have been using for thousands of years. Traditionally made from pure cotton wadding in either three or six layers (buy the latter for full-time use), futons offer natural insulation (so they're warm in winter and cool in summer), excellent support and considerable savings over an ordinary bed of comparable quality. Most are sold with a base of some kind (often slatted wood) to which you attach the rolled-up futon during the day

to make a sofa. Unlike conventional mattresses, futons positively benefit from being rolled up so the air can circulate around them to prevent mildew. Again, check the ease of this operation.

When you've explored all these possibilities, you may conclude that the most comfortable, best-looking and easiest sleeping arrangement in an all-purpose space is a simple divan, with a tailored cover in a hardwearing fabric. Treat it with a stain repellant like Scotchguard and add a huge bolster and plenty of throw cushions (including your pillows disguised in outer covers) to make an inviting sofa. For ease of making, use a fitted bottom sheet and a duvet, which you can hide away in the morning. You'll need a top-quality bed to fulfil this double function, and you should turn the mattress quite frequently so that you equalize wear.

Storage

Most one-room dwellers would prefer to feel they are sleeping in their living room rather than living in their bedroom, but this is the effect you'll create if there are clothes and toiletries constantly in evidence.

Think about devoting an entire wall to storage; at its cheapest (and perhaps its most charming) this could consist of shelves, hooks and hanging rails – perhaps even a basin or a tiny kitchen – concealed behind a dramatic sweep of floor-to-ceiling,

wall-to-wall curtains that are generously gathered and match those at the window. For a sleeker finish, fit blinds or cupboard doors here. You could even add a flap-down table to this kind of storage system.

For a unifying effect, fix a wide shelf at work-surface height across one wall – or all around the room – to provide a display area as well as storage capacity for books, records, plants, television, stereo, drinks tray, lamps, and anything that can be hidden in attractive boxes or baskets. In addition, it could act as a breakfast bar, sideboard and home office area.

A large chest of drawers (or several of them) offers generous surface space as well as capacious storage underneath. The top drawers will take cutlery, linen, paperwork, etc., while clothes can go in the lower, often larger ones.

Unless you're consistently neat,

LEFT *If you own more pictures and ornaments than you can accommodate, store some of them away, then rotate your displays so everything is on show at some time, and you get a periodic change of scene. Note how even the subtle change of floor level in this open-plan home makes the sleeping and sitting areas feel quite separate.*

FLAP TABLE AND STORAGE UNIT page 128

install a huge log basket in one corner into which you can toss all extraneous clutter for the inevitable emergency tidy-ups, then sort out the chaos when the panic is over.

For happy living in one room, some degree of personal discipline is vital, since one thing you don't have is the option to walk away from squalor; underclothes strewn around after a night on the town will look infinitely sordid and depressing the next morning.

Cooking

When you're faced with creating a kitchen as part of a larger room, you can choose ordinary freestanding appliances, install a permanent, built-in kitchen, or invest in an ingenious unit that combines fridge, sink and cooking facilities in one neat package and requires only the simplest plumbing and wiring.

If you're renting your one-room home and you have hopes of moving on to more spacious accommodation, investing in standard equipment you can take with you – even if it doesn't make the very best use of your present space – is probably the best idea. If you like, conceal the kitchen in one of the ways suggested earlier. When you own the property however, or you intend to stay there for the forseeable future, a completely built-in kitchen would be a good investment, not only because it looks neater, but also because appliances that are installed behind panels are considerably quieter than free-standing ones – a point to take into account if you think the unrelenting hum of a refrigerator will keep you awake nights. In addition of course, a beautifully designed and fitted kitchen will add considerably to the value of your property.

The third option – a kitchen-in-a-kit – comes into its own when you are equipping a bed-sitting room, maybe for an elderly relation or even for a lodger. Although these are expensive to buy, no structural work is needed to install them, and they are reasonably easy to transport if you want to use them elsewhere at some later date – in an office perhaps, or a holiday home.

Decorating

To prevent your overworked room from looking down-at-heel in a very short time, make sure all the surfaces – floors, walls, furniture – are tough enough to take the amount of wear they're going to get – and choose colours that don't show any

LEFT *You won't tire of a pale, neutral scheme, even when you're exposed to it constantly. For a change of view, choose different accent colours; yellow is the summer favourite in this attic studio, but red or black will give a completely new look when winter closes in.*

marks easily. Floors should be soft and comfortable underfoot, yet hardwearing and easy to clean, so avoid shaggy-pile carpets; cold, hard surfaces like ceramic tiles; and anything in a very pale colour.

If it's important in any small home that the walls and ceilings are simple and unobtrusive, this is even more true when that home consists of only one room – not only so the effect created will avoid being cluttered and fussy, but also to allow you to give yourself a sorely needed change of view by altering the less-expensive elements from time to time: cushions, tablecloths, lamps, pictures and so forth.

Be very sure of your chosen scheme before you begin to paint and do a very thorough job so you won't have to do it again for a long time. Decorating a one-room home can be a nightmare when you have to step over stacked-up furniture and assorted tins of paint for days on end, and there are few experiences less pleasant than trying to sleep in a room full of heavy fumes.

RIGHT *Exploit the restricted area under an attic window by putting your bed there – an especially good idea if you like to be awakened by streaming sunlight. Custom-built storage units follow the line of the ceiling to make full use of high-level space.*

This exotic eyrie is the London home of a widely travelled American businessman, who was willing to put up with its small, dark rooms because of their location in the heart of the city. The cool blue scheme he has selected not only makes the best of these natural disadvantages, it also provides an ideal display setting for his collection of American and African artefacts and textiles. He began by covering all the walls with a white base coat, then washed each room with a different intensity of his chosen colour, from the living room's dusky tone to the palest of tints in the bedroom and hall. The same soft, medium blue carpet was laid throughout, and slim white blinds replaced curtains at every window.

RIGHT *The tiny entrance hall appears to extend through a gracefully arched mirror hung at the end, whose shape echoes the decorative moulding above. The glass display shelves are practically invisible, whereas an ordinary piece of furniture would have looked clumsy.*

LEFT *When builders tried to demolish the partition wall that originally concealed the sloping ceiling, they discovered that the uprights inside it were supporting the roof. To avoid losing any precious space, these were disguised between a series of Moorish arches, then the wall behind was washed in a slightly darker shade so it appears to recede. Concealed lighting from a concealed spot makes the effect even more dramatic.*

RIGHT *Several classic small-space tactics have been used to make the kitchen look smart and function efficiently. An unbroken sweep of colour extends over the base units, across the work surface and up the splashback; set in the corner, a slim double sink is served by a neat, compact monobloc mixer tap. The existing cupboards were kept, but their bulky doors have been removed to give easy access.*

RIGHT *Fitted storage units were the only answer in the pocket-sized bedroom; mirrored door panels add space and light, and strengthen the visual impact of the intricate hanging and colourful patchwork quilts. The flat's blue theme is continued with a delicate border painted between two plain sections of moulding at the top of the almost-white walls.*

ABOVE *Another potentially awkward corner under the eaves has been turned into a storage/display area for audio equipment. Here again, the slope of the ceiling is accentuated rather than camouflaged by washing it with a much darker blue than the one used for the rest of the room.*

BELOW *Kitchen appliances are housed within a large curved bar faced with black laminate and topped with enamelled steel; behind this, mirrored cupboards hold crockery, plus cooking equipment and supplies. On the other side of the island unit, the bathroom and dressing room share space with a run of roomy closets.*

Living space in Manhattan is notoriously scarce, so even the few available apartments are likely to be severely restricted in size. Instead of dividing this top-floor loft into poky rooms, the architect who lives and works here has left it open, with only the bathroom and dressing area behind doors. The mauve and black colour treatment – an unusual one in a small space – is not oppressive because the windows are large and the aspect is a sunny, south-facing one. Laid throughout, black linoleum flooring is practical enough for office and kitchen use, and also provides an ideal background for rugs and carpets elsewhere.

BELOW *A work surface extending under the top of the bar offers plenty of room for preparing food and storing small appliances. Further capacity is provided by the cupboards and drawers, whose laminate finish and chrome handles are repeated in the bathroom and the corner devoted to the owner's architectural practice.*

BELOW The bath and toilet are concealed behind a partition wall, inset with translucent glass bricks to let in natural light; a neat sliding door affords privacy. Outside, the black basin is set into a vanity unit.

RIGHT The strong impression of light and space in the living area is mainly due to the huge expanses of window hung with full, floor-length curtains made from heavy artist's canvas.

BELOW RIGHT Positioned against a wall, a long table with a filing cabinet underneath acts as a desk; plans are drawn up at a drawing board set at right angles to it.

Most people's experience of living on a boat involves putting up with cramped, inconvenient accommodation for a limited period in order to enjoy a holiday on the open waves. The family who live on this delightfully converted Dutch barge, however, have made a roomy, comfortable and very pretty year-round home on a vessel that sees no other waters than those of the quiet English river where it's permanently moored. Although it originally had small berths for the boatman's family, the deep, flat-bottomed barge was mainly taken up with a huge cargo hold, and it is this space that now contains the family's main living and working area.

LEFT *To retain warmth, the boat's hull has waxed paper and fibreglass underneath the timber skin. Inside, there are sheets of plywood and thick tongue-and-groove boarding, with slatted ceilings resembling the original lift-off roof.*

FAR LEFT *With typical small-space ingenuity, the barge's owners have made sure that no surface around the bed has been wasted: a shelf above holds books, a wall-fixed spot provides light, and large lockers underneath offer valuable storage. Housed in an airing cupboard, the hot-water tank at its foot makes this curtained-off retreat especially cosy.*

LEFT *Echoing the shape of the box bed, the timber-framed bath can be hidden by a cane blind; a length of dowelling keeps towels handy. To warm the area, a slim radiator slots in where you'd expect to find a bath panel, and this is painted the same, typically Dutch, duck-egg blue as the rest of the room.*

ABOVE *Everything in the tiny galley is within easy reach of the wood-burning stove that provides heat and hot water as well as cooking facilities. Carefully positioned spotlights supplement the natural light sources. All available wall space is put to use for storage: prominently displayed, pieces of barge-painted china serve as almost the only reminder that this efficient country kitchen with its quarry-tiled floor is not on terra firma.*

ABOVE *A large cupboard in a small room has been camouflaged with the same red/grey marbled finish chosen for the walls. To supplement the bed-base drawers, simple hampers hold odds and ends.*

MAKING SPACE

Furniture and accessories that can be adapted for use in more than one way are often difficult to find and expensive to buy, but customized pieces can be constructed using only basic carpentry skills. Copy the projects in this section, combine and adapt elements from several of them, or use our ideas to spark off your own solutions to small-space problems.

This section contains 20 designs for items of furniture and accessories that will help you make the best possible use of the space you have. They can be adapted for use in different sizes and situations, and made up in a wide variety of materials and finishes to suit any decorating style.

For a bright, informal scheme or in a children's room, choose chipboard, blockboard or plywood, varnished, painted or covered in tough laminate, which comes in a huge range of neutral, pastel and primary colours. You could even experiment with contrast edging or colourful knobs and handles. In sleek, sophisticated rooms, one of the above boards with a veneer face, left natural or stained black, would come into its own, sealed with a coat of polyurethane and set off with elegant brass or chrome fittings. To give shelves a quality look, use extra thick timber, or add a deeper edging to achieve a similar effect.

Don't be afraid to adapt our designs freely, making them simpler or adding extra features according to your needs. Alternatively, combine elements from several different projects to arrive at the optimum solution to the particular problems you are facing.

This is essentially an ideas section; the drawings on the following pages are meant simply to provide a rough assembly plan. There are no detailed step-by-step instructions, so if you aren't familiar with the relevant techniques, consult a good do-it-yourself manual, or discuss the projects you're attracted to with a professional carpenter who can make them up for you. Even when you are not able to undertake any construction yourself, make sure the final result is exactly what you had in mind by researching thoroughly all the materials and the practical and decorative fittings available, then discussing your preferences with the carpenter or cabinet maker you've employed.

PAGE 124 *Conceal the sleeping arrangements in a bedsitter or studio during the day, by tucking them away under a low platform piled high with cushions.*

MULTI-PURPOSE COFFEE TABLE

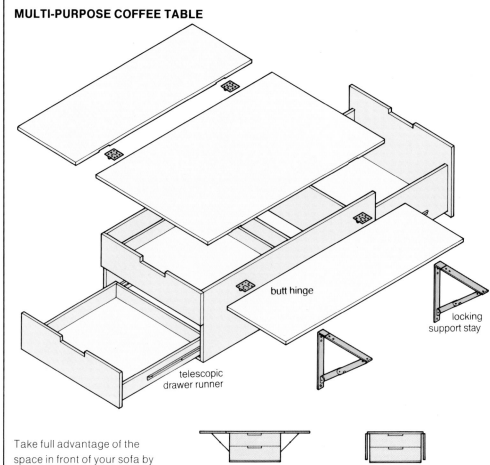

butt hinge

locking support stay

telescopic drawer runner

Take full advantage of the space in front of your sofa by installing this ingenious coffee table, which has an extending top and roomy storage underneath.

Pull up the flaps along either side when you want to use the table for low, Japanese-style dining or family games. We have shown two shallow drawers and one deep one, but you can choose your own arrangement, depending on whether they're to be used for china and cutlery, bottles and glasses, papers and files, or playing cards and board games.

Support the flaps with lockable stays, and be sure to extend the main tabletop far enough over the sides to accommodate the stays. If your drawers are to contain heavy items like bottles, china or cutlery, fit them with telescopic runners.

CONSOLE TABLE

Perfect for a hall or landing as well as a pint-sized room, this slim and stylish console table takes up very little room against a wall and makes a useful display area or desk.

When you need a larger top, to serve as a dining table for entertaining perhaps, or as a work surface for sewing or model making, simply unfold top and base sections to double the table's capacity.

Its measurements will depend on your space and your requirements, but a chipboard table should not be larger than about 46 × 183cm (18in × 6ft) for maximum strength. Plywood or blockboard versions can be made in larger sizes, as long as the thickness of the board is increased appropriately.

Piano hinges are the easiest to fix and the cheapest to buy; counter hinges cost more and are trickier to install, but they give a much neater effect and are available with a decorative chrome or brass finish.

Attach the surface to the base with nylon, plastic or wooden joint blocks, or with shrinkage plates.

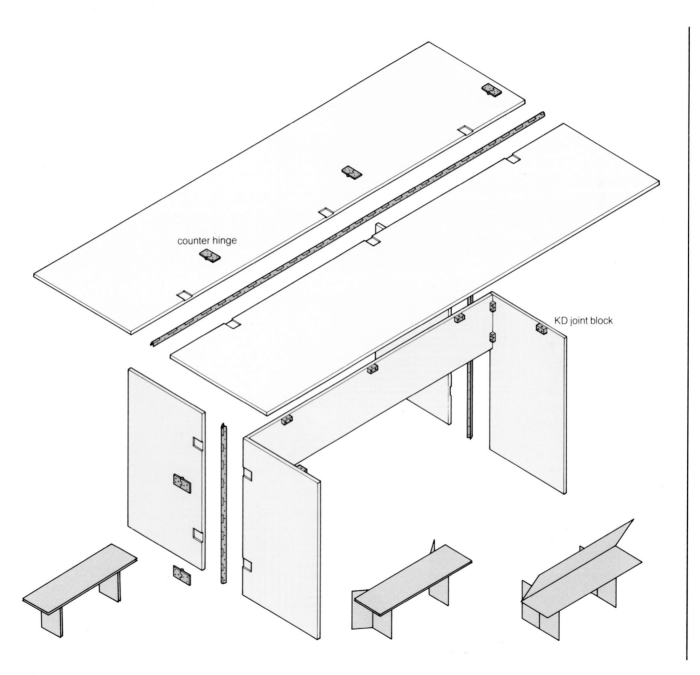

counter hinge

KD joint block

FLAP TABLE AND STORAGE UNIT

This neat table-plus-storage unit can be squeezed into the tightest corner to provide dining, desk, or hobby facilities that you might otherwise have to do without. Choose a flap-down surface to conceal some or all of the shelves, or a flap-up one if you want to have constant access to them.

For **A**, fix the surface to the bottom of the storage unit with a sturdy piano hinge, and attach the legs to the underside with lockable stays. In the 'up' position, the surface is safely anchored with turn buttons.

For **B**, support the table with a simple gateleg mechanism so it folds flat against the wall when it's not in use. A small, semi-circular version could provide much needed space for breakfasts and quick snacks, invaluable in a tiny kitchen.

To achieve the warm, mellow look of an old-fashioned dresser or hutch, use second-hand rather than new wood. Planed-up floorboards would be ideal for shelves, and you may be able to salvage timber from an unwanted piece of furniture for the table.

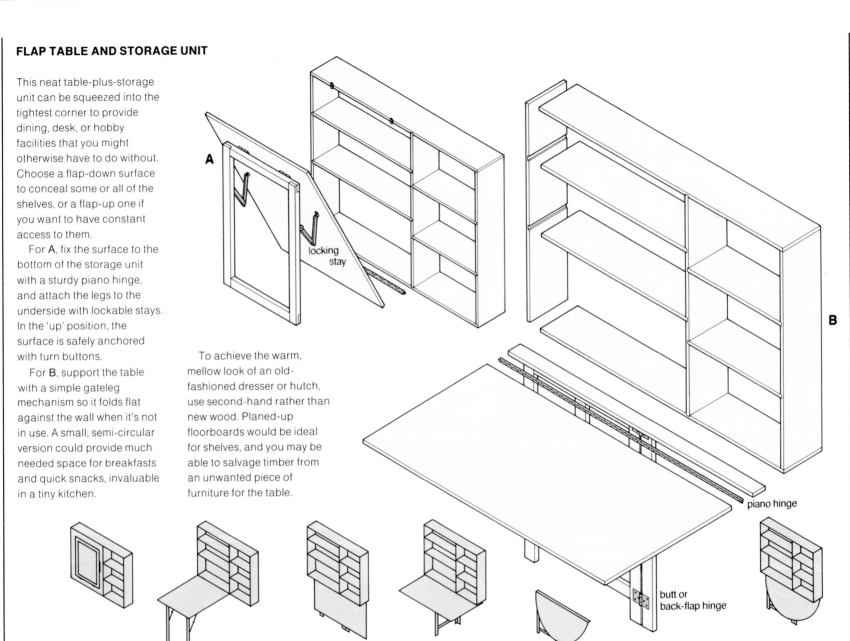

A

locking stay

B

piano hinge

butt or back-flap hinge

DUAL-HEIGHT TABLE

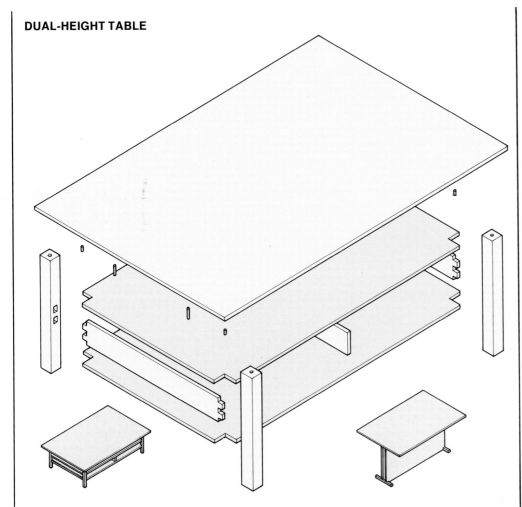

CORNER FLAP TABLE

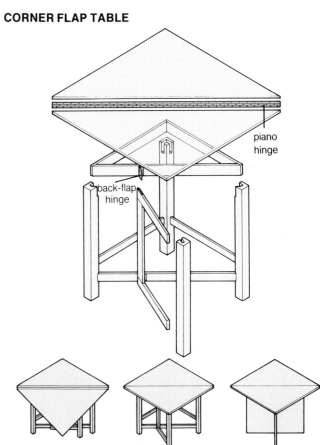

piano hinge

back-flap hinge

Even when you can do without a dining table on a day-to-day basis, it's nice to be able to serve formal meals once in a while. By simply lifting the top off this low coffee table, upending the base, and slotting the top back, you can change its height in seconds. A neat dowel arrangement anchors the two sections together; use slightly longer dowels for the dining version.

The stability of this structure comes from the mortice and tenon joints used to assemble the box base, so don't substitute an easier construction method. Also to ensure maximum strength, you should avoid using chipboard for this design.

The traditional gateleg structure adapts very easily to stylish, modern designs. This square model, hinged diagonally across the middle, tucks literally into a corner. Extend its leaf, and you have a desk or an eating place for one or two; pulled out into the room, it can seat four.

Use piano or butt hinges for the top, or more complex but unobtrusive back flap ones. Make sure the leg assembly is set back far enough to accommodate the gate leg, which you could make up from dowels, or even from flat board, fitting a piano hinge for the flap.

CORNER OFFICE

flush-fitting
retaining bolt

locking
stay

butt hinges

Every household should have a place where the business of running a home can be carried on, paperwork filed and letters written. Just by attaching a pair of doors to a simple corner-fixed framework, you can provide an efficient and compact home office, study or hobby area that can be closed off completely when it's not being used. A grid storage system could also be fitted above the work surface. Add a flap-down table if you need a larger work surface that wouldn't otherwise fit into your room.

Construct the doors yourself, or buy ready-made louvres. If these are not tall enough to reach from floor to ceiling, fix them only above the height of the work surface, or install two sets that are either opened separately or fixed together to operate as one set.

If you include the flap-down table, make sure there is enough space between the underside of the top in the 'up' position and the doors so they can close completely. Secure in position with a flush-fitting retaining bolt.

PLATFORM STORAGE

One of the subtlest ways to define areas within a room is with a change of level. This low platform, covered to

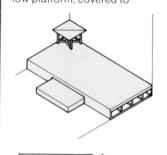

match the floor covering, also provides storage facilities by way of lift-up flaps, drawers, or a trundle bed.

Construct the decking from floorboards or flooring-grade chipboard or plywood. If you choose these, ensure each joint has studwork underneath. To accommodate a bed, use thicker support timbers as compensation for the lost uprights.

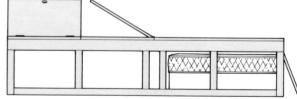

TRUNDLE BED

One of the oldest space-saving ideas in existence, trundle (or truckle) beds have been around since the fifteenth century, when smaller, servants' beds pulled out from under the master's larger one.

In undersized modern homes, this arrangement will sleep two small children in the same room while leaving space for play during the day, or allow a single occupant to entertain an overnight visitor. A trundle bed in the parents' room would provide temporary accommodation for a child while the nursery is being used as a guest room.

The design should be constructed from timber. Be sure to measure the mattresses carefully before you start (they can be the same size) so the frame will fit.

The trundle can be pulled to another part of the room since it is on castors; fix a set in the centre of the box section as well as at each end for additional support. If the floor is hard and smooth, you may need lockable ones. To store bedding, fit drawers in the side on telescopic runners.

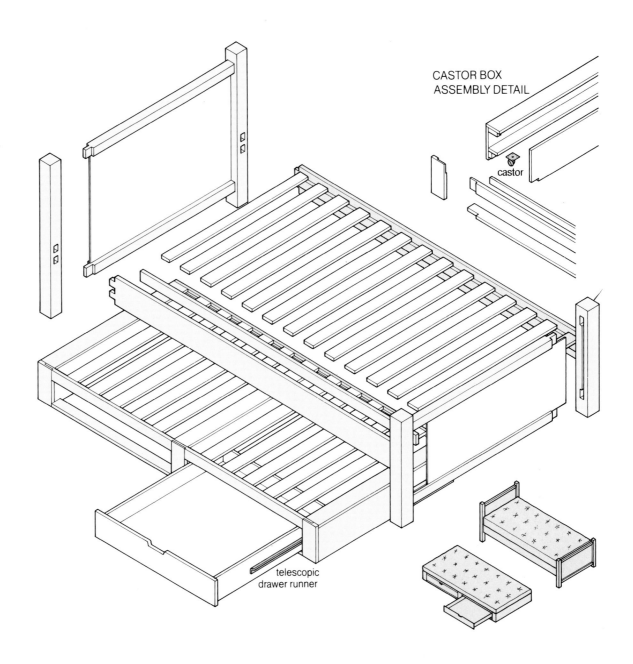

CASTOR BOX
ASSEMBLY DETAIL

castor

telescopic
drawer runner

PLATFORM BED

Another sensible sleeping arrangement when space is tight is a platform bed, raised high enough to make room for another bed (forming traditional bunks), a desk, or even hanging clothes storage (not shown) underneath.

Using blockboard, ply or timber (chipboard is not strong enough), make four leg sections and one or two sub-frames. With coach bolts, attach the sub-frames to the legs, or the desk section to the frame.

For flexibility, drill holes in the leg sections at several heights so the level of the bed or work surface can be adjusted. Use the same pre-drilled, home-made jig each time to make sure the holes align with the sub-frame.

Using a similar, but simpler, construction, you could build a work station at the end of a single-tier bed, with a simple hinged panel that lifts up to form the desktop.

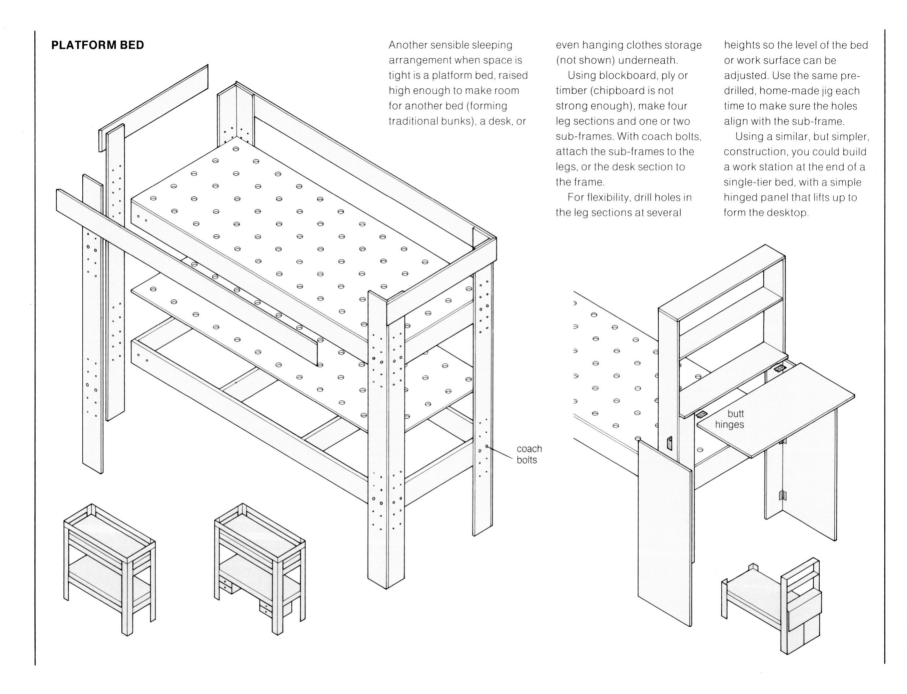

coach bolts

butt hinges

MODULAR FURNISHING SYSTEM

Custom-made, fitted furniture often uses space most efficiently, but it is costly to buy and cannot be moved around or taken with you when you move, like freestanding pieces.

To get the best of both worlds, design and make a modular system that can be combined in many different ways and shifted around easily for use in an adult's or child's bedroom, or in a one-room flat or apartment.

Ours is based on multiples of 50cm (20in), which is about half the width of our single bed. All the storage items have this unit as their depth, and the cubes are this wide as well, whereas the bookcase/desk and the wardrobe are 1m (40in) wide.

Details for the bed storage drawers and the flap-up work surface appear elsewhere in this section. When making the drawer unit for the wardrobe, construct a separate drawer assembly to provide enough clearance so that they open easily.

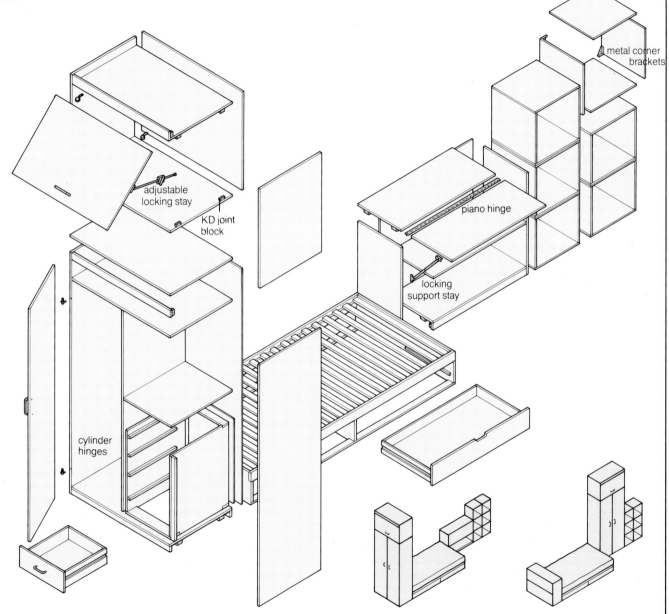

metal corner brackets

adjustable locking stay

KD joint block

piano hinge

locking support stay

cylinder hinges

CHOPPING BOARD AND KNIFE RACK

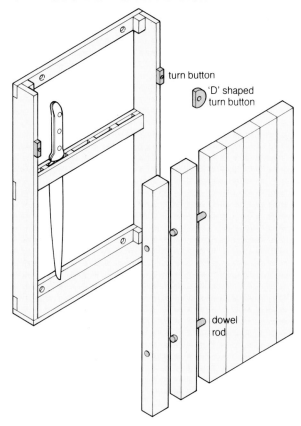

turn button

'D' shaped
turn button

dowel
rod

Your kitchen will function most efficiently when the work surface is clear, and often-used equipment is stored close by. Make use of the area between the counter and the cupboards by fixing this wall-hung chopping board that lifts away easily for use and conceals a slotted rack to keep your knives handy, sharp and safe.

Use solid, seasoned timber that will not warp in the heat and damp of the kitchen; you might be able to salvage this from an unwanted piece of furniture. Hold the board in place with simple turn buttons, and fix spacers in the rack to keep knives straight and separate.

STACKING BOXES

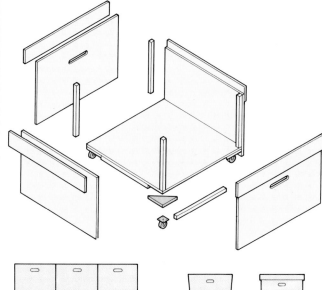

Sort out storage problems with a set of roomy boxes that stack on top of each other to take up minimal space, and roll out of sight on castors. In a child's room, they would be invaluable for toys; you could even identify their contents with colour coding (blue for games, red for dolls and stuffed animals, and so forth). Fill them with boots and bags in an adult's bedroom, or use them to bring order to the chaos in an attic or basement storage area.

Our construction method involves simple corner fillet fixing, but for a neater inside finish, you could rebate the corners and house the base section into the sides. If your chosen material is ply, add extra support for the castors. Make your boxes stackable either by fixing lipping at the top as shown, or by tapering the bottom.

WINE-GLASS HOLDER

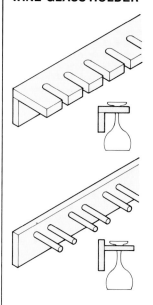

Make use of wasted space under a shelf – perhaps inside a cupboard – by fixing a handy, solid-timber rack for your stemmed glasses that also protects them from damage. (Glasses should never be stored face down on a shelf, since the rim is the weakest part.)

Using the same principle, but enlarging the rack and increasing the spaces between the hanging sections, you could also make a useful holder for garden or carpentry tools, or for long-handled cleaning equipment like mops, brooms and brushes.

ALCOVE SHELF WITH DRAWERS

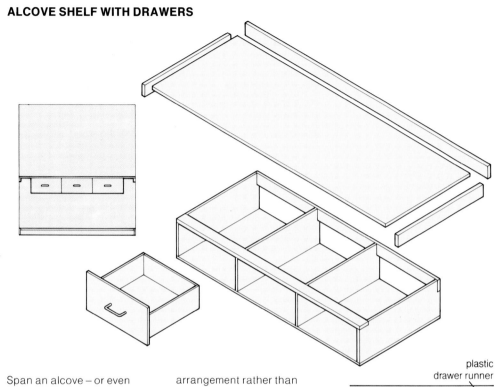

Span an alcove – or even one end of a small room – with a deep, sturdy work surface that has a row of drawers hung underneath. In a living or dining room, this could do double duty, as a home office or study area when needed, and as a sideboard at mealtimes. Cutlery and table linen can be stored in one drawer, writing materials and paperwork in another. Similarly, it could serve as a desk and a dressing table in the bedroom. Using this arrangement rather than freestanding furniture not only makes efficient use of space, it also increases the apparent size of the room since the floor is left clear.

It's important that you compensate for uneven walls by constructing a square framework for the drawers to run on. Or choose wire baskets or plastic storage bins instead, both of which operate on runners fixed to the underside of the shelf.

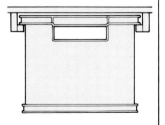

plastic drawer runner

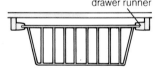

SUSPENDED SHELVES

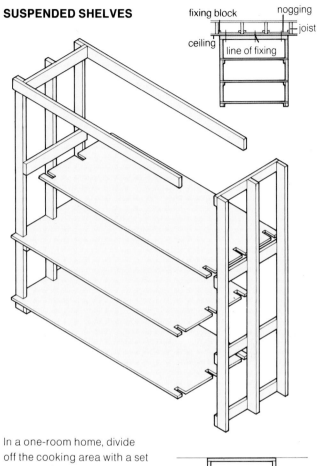

fixing block   nogging   joist
ceiling   line of fixing

In a one-room home, divide off the cooking area with a set of open shelves suspended from the ceiling above a peninsular or island unit. These shelves will hold pretty china, or rows of glasses that let through the maximum amount of light.

To create a stable fixing, you may have to locate additional timbers between existing joists.

SLIDING SHELF UNIT

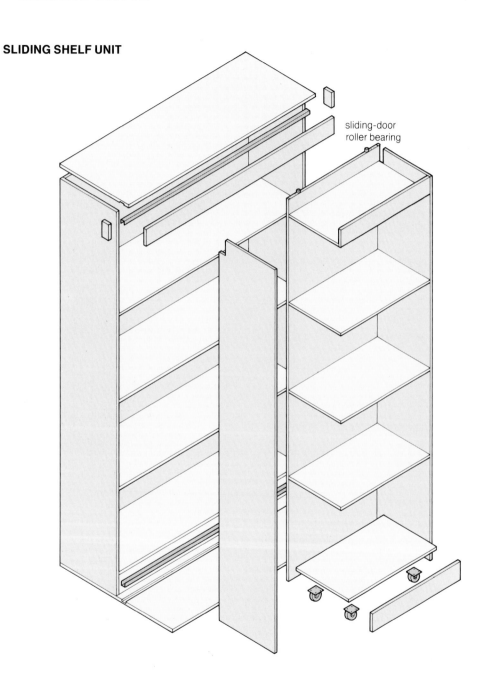

sliding-door
roller bearing

When there isn't enough wall space to accommodate all the shelves you need, increase your storage capacity by building a box shelf unit, then anchoring an additional half-width one in front, which can be moved to gain access. The shelves are designed to function as a one-piece unit with the base of the rear section providing a stable platform on which the castors for the front section can run.

As a library system, it would hold half again as many books as an ordinary run of shelves. In the kitchen you could store a great deal of extra equipment and supplies, and in a child's or teenager's room, a growing collection of bulky toys and sports equipment could be kept off the floor.

The half-width unit operates on the same principle as a sliding door, and uses the same mechanism to hold it in position. This is not weight bearing however – the four castors on which the unit moves provide its support.

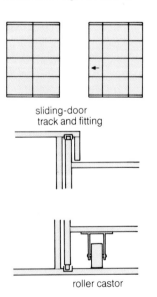

sliding-door
track and fitting

roller castor

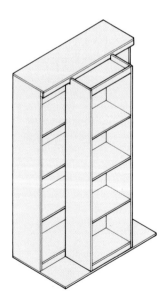

PULL-OUT LARDER SHELVES

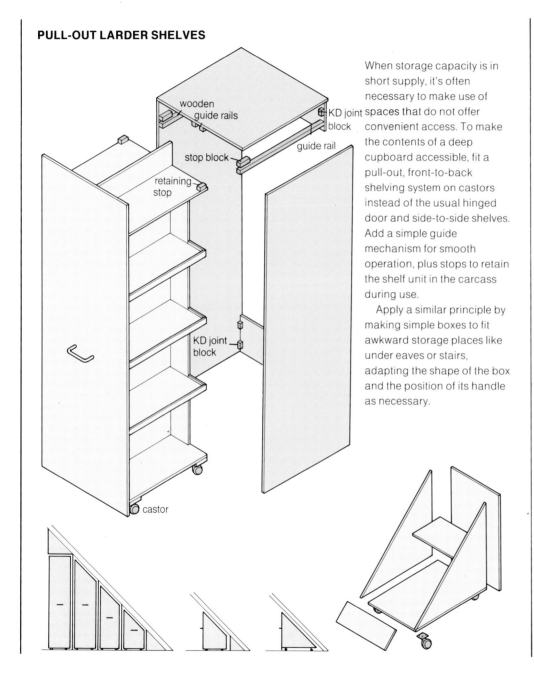

wooden
guide rails

KD joint
block

guide rail

stop block

retaining
stop

KD joint
block

castor

When storage capacity is in short supply, it's often necessary to make use of spaces that do not offer convenient access. To make the contents of a deep cupboard accessible, fit a pull-out, front-to-back shelving system on castors instead of the usual hinged door and side-to-side shelves. Add a simple guide mechanism for smooth operation, plus stops to retain the shelf unit in the carcass during use.

Apply a similar principle by making simple boxes to fit awkward storage places like under eaves or stairs, adapting the shape of the box and the position of its handle as necessary.

SLIDE-OUT WORK SURFACE

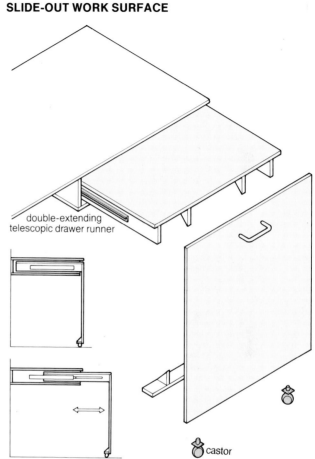

double-extending
telescopic drawer runner

castor

Supplement a small work surface with a right-angled extension that pulls out easily on telescopic drawer runners when it's needed, then tucks away completely afterwards. Since the unit is constructed with a solid frontpiece and castors underneath, it will bear considerable weight, so you could use it for a typewriter or word processor, or for several small appliances in the kitchen. Note the additional support on the castor assembly.

SCREENS AND SHUTTERS

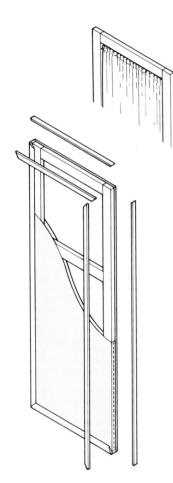

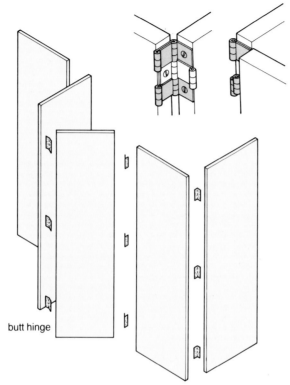

butt hinge

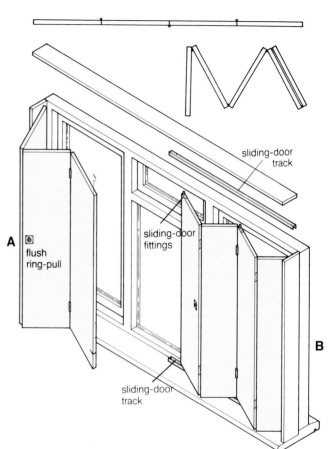

sliding-door
track

sliding-door
fittings

A

flush
ring-pull

sliding-door
track

B

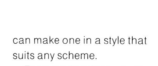

One of the most effective and flexible means of dividing space, screens are basically only three or more hinged frames, made from lightweight timber held together with dowel joints. By altering the decoration, you

can make one in a style that suits any scheme.

For a modern look, staple striking fabric flat to the top and side faces of each panel, then conceal the staples with timber edging or a strip of coloured tape. For a pretty, old-fashioned effect, gather the fabric before you staple it, or fix horizontal dowels at the top and bottom of each frame on which the fabric can be

gathered. Alternatively, clad both sides with board, then paint them or cover them with cork to make a pinboard – or use sheets of ply, and jig out a simple pattern.

To assemble the panels, use paravent hinges, which open both ways, or the more conventional butt hinges, which must be fixed on alternate sides (as shown).

Make neat, space-saving

shutters in the same way, fixing them inside a simple timber frame. Choose those with gathered fabric for a softening effect. If there are more than four narrow, or three wide, panels, anchor them top and bottom with a sliding-door mechanism (B).

CONSERVATORY WINDOW

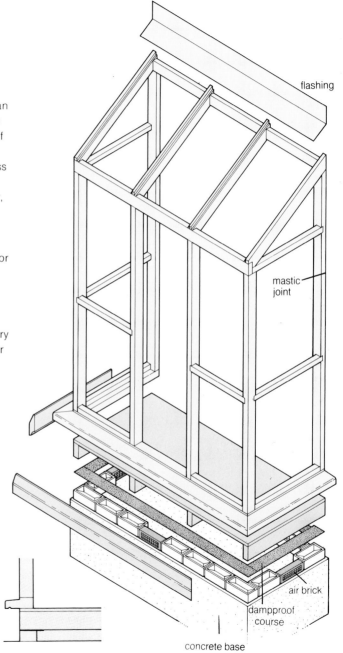

To accommodate plants when you have no garden, build a small greenhouse onto an ordinary window. If the window is a sash, you can leave it in place; if it intrudes into your plants' space – or if you want them to be part of your room – remove the glass and glazing bars.

Use only seasoned timber, suitably treated and primed with preservative. The frame must be weatherproofed where it joins the building. For ventilation, fit louvre units in the side panels and/or drill holes in the supporting platform.

To add a mini-conservatory to a doorway, install a similar frame on a specially-prepared base, around ready-made doors.

If these structures are not built and installed correctly, moisture can seep in and cause extensive damage, so unless you are very experienced, seek expert advice.

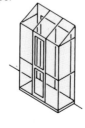

flashing

mastic joint

air brick

dampproof course

concrete base

INDEX

Numbers in italics refer to illustration captions

ACKNOWLEDGMENTS

1 Shona Wood (Wendy Shillam & Michael Robertson-Smith architects); **2** World of Interiors/ Tom Leighton; **7** Jean-Paul Bonhommet; **8** Michael Boys; **9–10** Jean-Paul Bonhommet; **12** Shona Wood (Charles Rutherfoord); **13** Jean-Paul Bonhommet; **14** Michael Boys; **15** Marcus Harrison; **16** left Arcaid/Tim Soar; **16** right Shona Wood (Charles Rutherfoord); **17** Richard Paul; **18** Arcaid/Richard Bryant; **19** Rodney Hyett/EWA; **20** Guy Bouchet; **21** Marcus Harrison; **22** Michael Nicholson/EWA; **23** left Shona Wood (Holland/Hyatt); **23** right Spike Powell/EWA; **24** Andreas von Einsiedel/EWA; **25** above Marcus Harrison; **25** below Dulux; **26** above Homes & Gardens/Syndication International; **26** below Spike Powell/EWA; **27** Homes & Gardens/Syndication International; **28** Michael Boys; **29** left Spike Powell/EWA; **29** right Arcaid/Richard Bryant; **30** Tim Street-Porter/EWA; **31** left Richard Paul; **31** right Di Lewis/EWA; **32** Camera Press; **33** La Maison de Marie Claire (Girardeau/Hirsch-Marie); **34** Ken Kirkwood; **35** La Maison de Marie Claire (Nicholas/ Postic) **36** Jerry Tubby/EWA; **37** left Michael Boys; **37** right Carol Yuan/EWA; **38** Michael Dunne/EWA; **39** Ianthe Ruthven; **40–43** Ken Kirkwood (Mr & Mrs David Hillman); **44** Fritz von der Schulenburg; **46** Rodney Hyett/EWA; **47** World of Interiors/Fritz von der Schulenburg; **48** World of Interiors/David Montgomery; **49** Simon Brown (Ian Hutchinson architect); **50** Homes & Gardens/Syndication International; **51** left Vivian Boje; **51** right Spike Powell/EWA; **52** Michael Dunne/EWA; **53** Ken Kirkwood; **54** La Maison de Marie Claire (Hussenot); **55** Michael Dunne/EWA; **56** Shona Wood (Wendy Shillam & Malcolm Robertson-Smith architects); **57** Ken Kirkwood; **58** Arcaid/Richard Bryant; **59** Antoine Rozès; **60** left Bulthaup; **60** right Pat Hunt; **61** Guy Bouchet; **62** Camera Press; **63** left World of Interiors/Clive Frost; **63** right Shona Wood (Wendy Shillam & Malcolm Robertson-Smith architects); **64** left Jean-Paul Bonhommet; **64** right SieMatic; **65** Ken Kirkwood; **66** left ELFA; **66** right Jean-Paul Bonhommet; **67** Simon Brown (Angela and Jerry Hewitt); **68** Rodney Hyett/EWA; **69** Jean-Paul Bonhommet; **70** Rodney Hyett/EWA; **71** Shona Wood (Wendy Shillam & Malcolm Robertson-Smith architects); **72** Jon Bouchier/EWA; **73** Michael Dunne/EWA; **74** Camera Press; **75** World of Interiors/Fritz von der Schulenburg; **76** above Good Housekeeping/Tom Leighton; **76** below Homes & Gardens/Syndication International; **77** Michael Dunne/EWA; **78** left Camera Press; **78** right Good Housekeeping/David Brittain; **79** World of Interiors/Clive Frost; **80** Rodney Hyett/EWA; **81** Camera Press; **82** above Michael Crockett/EWA; **82** below Camera Press; **83** Jean-Paul Bonhommet; **84** left Andreas von Einsiedel/EWA; **84** right Annet Held; **85** Richard Paul; **86** World of Interiors/Tim Beddow; **87** World of Interiors/Fritz von der Schulenburg; **88** Shona Wood (fashion designer Stephen King); **89** Jean-Paul Bonhommet; **90** Camera Press; **91** above Michael Boys; **91** below Dulux; **92** La Maison de Marie Claire (Korniloff); **93** Camera Press; **94** Arcaid/ Lucinda Lambton; **95** World of Interiors/Clive Frost; **96** Simon Brown; **97** World of Interiors/ James Mortimer; **98** left Dragons of Walton Street; **98** right Michael Nicholson/EWA; **99** Simon Brown (Robert T Bayley architect); **100** Rodney Hyett/EWA; **101** Garry Chowanetz/EWA; **102** Rodney Hyett/EWA; **103** left Abitare/Christine Tiberghien; **103** right Arcaid/Lucinda Lambton; **104–105** Andreas von Einsiedel/Good Housekeeping (Simon Child architect); **105** Camera Press; **106** left Abitare/Gabriele Basilico; **106** right Jean-Paul Bonhommet; **107** Vivian Boje; **108–109** Conran Foundation; **110** Jean-Paul Bonhommet; **111** Michael Dunne/EWA; **112–113** Camera Press; **114** La Maison de Marie Claire (Pataut); **115** Camera Press; **116** Abitare/Christine Tiberghien; **117** Camera Press; **118–119** Shona Wood (Jonathan Bartlett interior designer); **120–121** Simon Brown (Ed Carroll architect); **122–123** Spike Powell/EWA; **124** Camera Press

LIST OF SUPPLIERS

The following companies can either provide a list of stockists for the items listed, or supply them direct.

spiral stairs
Albion Design of Cambridge Limited
12 Flitcroft Street
London WC2H 8DJ
(will dispatch to any destination in the UK or overseas)

radiators
Bisque
244 Belsize Road
London NW6 4BT
(suppliers of a huge range of modern and traditional designs that can be dispatched anywhere in the UK)

Microfurnace (thermostatically controlled freestanding heater)

Micromar UK Limited	Micromar International
29 Douglas Street	RR1
Milngavie	Orono
Glasgow G62 6PE	Ontario
Scotland	Canada

wire storage baskets

Elfa Domestic Storage Systems	Elfa Corporation of America
Penallta Industrial Estate	Princeton Professional Park
Ystrad Mynach	Suite B7
Mid Glamorgan CF8 7QZ	601 Ewing Street
	Princeton
	New Jersey 08540

wall grid storage-system and clip-on baskets

Habitat	Conran's
at branches or by mail order from:	at branches or by mail order from:
Habitat Designs Limited	Conran's Mail Order
PO Box 2	CN 2103
Wallingford	Lakewood
Oxfordshire OX10 9DQ	New Jersey 08701-1053

small flap-down table

Habitat (UK)	Conran's (US)
	addresses as above

nesting tables

Habitat (UK)	Conran's (US)
	addresses as above

small deep bath
Mantaleda Bathrooms
Leeming Bar Industrial Estate
Northallerton
North Yorks DL7 9DH

child's platform bed with storage underneath

Habitat (UK)	Conran's (US)
	addresses as above

single unit kitchens

Dahl Bros Limited	Gustavsberg
Scandia Works	Gustavsberg
Armfield Close, Molesey Avenue	Sweden
East Molesey	(Scandia Kitchen Centre – will dispatch
Surrey KT8 OJS	overseas)
(Scandia Kitchen Centre)	

Kitchen equipment
The companies listed manufacture a range of items of interest to the small space dweller; particularly specialized designs are mentioned after each entry. In general, European appliances sold in the US and Canada are considerably smaller than those made in North America.

Ariston Domestic Appliances Limited	**Ariston Domestic Appliances**
Ariston House	Acme National Sales Company
London Road	99 West Hawthorne Avenue
High Wycombe	Valley Stream
Buckinghamshire HP11 1BQ	New York N.Y.
(countertop dishwasher 700S)	

ASEA Appliances
ASEA House
36 The Butts
Brentford
Middlesex TW8 8BL
(benchtop dishwasher 750)

T.I. Creda Limited
Creda Works
PO Box 5
Blythe Bridge
Stoke-on-Trent ST11 9LJ
(slimline hobs, including ceramic;
combination ovens; small tumbler drier
that can be wall hung; plinth-mounted
fan heater)

Creda
72 Chase Drive
Sharon
Massachusetts 02067
(slimline cook-tops, gas or electric,
including ceramic; double or single
electric convection ovens)

Franke UK
Suite 15B
Manchester International Office Centre
Styal Road
Manchester M22 5UB
(compact and double sinks and
accessories)

Franke Inc.
Kitchen Systems Division
2321 North Penn Road
PO Box 4–8
Hatfield
Pennsylvania 19440

Hobart Manufacturing Company
Hobart House
51 The Bourne
Southgate
London N14 6RT
(waste disposal units; rubbish
compactor)

Hobart Corporation
Troy
Ohio 45374
(food waste disposers; trash
compactor)

Husqvarna
PO Box 10
Oakley Road
Luton LU4 9QW
(Minette countertop dishwasher)

The Miele Company Limited
Fairacres Trading Estate
Marcham Road
Abingdon
Oxfordshire
OX14 1TW
(top-loading washer/drier WT489)

Miele Appliances Inc.
22D World's Fair Drive
Somerset
New Jersey 08873

Philips Electronics
City House
420–430 London Road
Croydon
Surrey CR9 3QR
(under-counter refrigerators and
freezers; small tumble drier)

The North American Philips
Organization
100 East 42nd Street
New York N.Y. 10017

Zanussi Limited
Zanussi House
Hanbridge Road
Newbury
Berkshire RG14 5EP
(microwave that fixes under a wall
cupboard; compact, under-counter
refrigerators and freezers; top-loading
washer TL1033)

The Zanussi Corporation of America
One World Trade Centre
New York N.Y. 10048

Special needs
The following organizations will provide information on equipping a home for an
elderly or handicapped person.

Disabled Living Foundation
380–384 Harrow Road
London W9 2HU

Centre on Environment for the Handicapped
35 Great Smith Street
London SW1P 3BJ

National Institute of Senior Housing
A Division of the National Council on the Ageing Inc.
600 Maryland Avenue SW
West Wing 100
Washington DC 20024

American National Standards Institute
1430 Broadway
New York N.Y. 10018
(This organization publishes a useful booklet called *American National Standard
for Buildings and Facilities Providing Accessibility and Useability for Physically
Handicapped People*. Order No ANSI A117.1–1986. Price on application.)